Language Contact and Vocabulary Enrichment

STUDIES IN ENGLISH MEDIEVAL LANGUAGE AND LITERATURE

Edited by Jacek Fisiak

Advisory Board:
John Anderson (Methoni, Greece), Ulrich Busse (Halle),
Olga Fischer (Amsterdam), Dieter Kastovsky (Vienna),
Marcin Krygier (Poznań), Roger Lass (Cape Town),
Peter Lucas (Cambridge), Donka Minkova (Los Angeles),
Akio Oizumi (Kyoto), Katherine O'Brien O'Keeffe (UC Berkeley, USA),
Matti Rissanen (Helsinki), Hans Sauer (Munich),
Liliana Sikorska (Poznań), Jeremy Smith (Glasgow),
Jerzy Wełna (Warsaw)

Vol. 34

PETER LANG
Frankfurt am Main · Berlin · Bern · Bruxelles · New York · Oxford · Warszawa · Wien

Isabel Moskowich

Language Contact and Vocabulary Enrichment

Scandinavian Elements in Middle English

PETER LANG
Internationaler Verlag der Wissenschaften

Bibliographic Information published by the Deutsche Nationalbibliothek
The Deutsche Nationalbibliothek lists this publication in the Deutsche Nationalbibliografie; detailed bibliographic data is available in the internet at http://dnb.d-nb.de.

The publication was financially supported
by the Universidad de Coruña,
Department of English Philology.

Cover design:
© Olaf Glöckler, Atelier Platen, Friedberg

Typesetting by motivex.

ISSN 1436-7521
ISBN 978-3-631-62414-2
© Peter Lang GmbH
Internationaler Verlag der Wissenschaften
Frankfurt am Main 2012
All rights reserved.

All parts of this publication are protected by copyright. Any utilisation outside the strict limits of the copyright law, without the permission of the publisher, is forbidden and liable to prosecution. This applies in particular to reproductions, translations, microfilming, and storage and processing in electronic retrieval systems.

www.peterlang.de

Contents

Introduction 7

Chapter One: The historical context 15
   1. Some preliminary considerations 15
   2. Causes for the Scandinavian expansion 17
   3. The Scandinavians in England: the Danelaw 21
   4. The Second Migration 32
   5. Types of Scandinavian settlements in England 36

Chapter Two: The social structure 41
   1. Social organisation in pre-Norse times 41
   2. Social organisation of the field in non-Scandinavian areas 49
   3. Society and the economy in the Danelaw. Scandinavian influence in the social fabric 52
   4. Towns and commercial activity 58

Chapter Three: The sociolinguistic perspective and related studies 61
   1. Introduction 61
   2. Three fundamental models 61
   3. Speech community 71
   4. Language contact 72
   5. Bilingualism and diglossia 74
   6. Pidgins and creoles 83
   7. A brief overview of lexical change 86

Chapter Four: The corpus 89
   1. Plan and method 89
   2. Meanings 91
   3. Dates 92
   4. Citing texts 92
   5. Grammatical categories 94
   6. Etymology 95

7.	Dialects	95
8.	Semantic fields	96
9.	Spelling	96

Chapter Five: The lexical system of Scandinavian England 99
1.	Introduction	99
2.	Dates	99
3.	Dialects	104
4.	Semantic fields	110
5.	Text-types	123
6.	Grammatical categories	126

Chapter Six: Some final remarks 133

Appendix 141
1.	Manuscripts and manuscript collections	141
2	Periodicals, series and Festschriften	145

References 151

Introduction

A number of significant works on the history of the English language have appeared in recent years. *The Cambridge History of English* (1992-2001) and *The Oxford History of English* (2006), for example, aim at presenting the history of English as a continuum, in contrast to the somewhat fragmented views we are more accustomed to see. The Anglocentric perspective still dominates the scene, as is the case in both of the above texts. Many authors, though, approach the development of English in different ways and from more dynamic perspectives, in which extra-systemic factors are especially relevant. As Townend (2010: 61) notes, "one cannot look at English in isolation; for much of its history the English language in England has been in a state of coexistence, competition, or even conflict with one or more other languages". It is with this in mind that the current book has evolved, focussing on a particular point in the evolution of the English lexicon.

The concept of lexical availability was introduced some years ago (Bernstein 1961; Samper Padilla 2006: 101), and refers to the inventory of thematically-related words that a speaker can draw on without undue or excessive effort. In this sense, speakers of English have at their disposal an extensive range of lexical items. However, when they turn to the available lexicon, searching for a particular word, they seldom consider the origins of each available lexical item. Of central interest in this book will be the development of the lexicon which is, or at least once was, available in English. The approach, rather than being cognitive, will adopt the perspective arising from the relation between a language and its speakers over the course of time. Indeed, as Braunmüller and House (2009: 2) have pointed out, the study of language contact itself stems from historical linguistics, and for this reason I believe that history must be taken into account here.

It is generally agreed that certain areas of England were visited and settled by Norsemen from the late eighth century onwards. However, scholarly debate has raged for years as to the social ranks of these newcomers, how big their clans were, and as to whether they were simply warriors and raiders or if the whole process might be regarded as migration. Contemporary documents often mention hostile attitudes on the part of these "visitors", who were generally not welcome. A text such as the *Parker Chronicle*, for example, with its inexact chronology (see below) is an extremely valuable source in that it describes aspects of these historical events, based not on Latin records, but rather on the vernacular.

The present volume has resorted both to primary and secondary sources. The different known versions of the *Anglo-Saxon Chronicle* have been compared, and the comparison has been complemented with historiographical works. An important part of the analysis is based on relevant secondary sources such as the *Middle English Dictionary* (Kurath et al. 1956-1963, hereafter *MED*), which has been used here as a source of corpus data due to its reliability and its unequalled quality as a reference work. The use of material from the *MED* with the aim of better understanding Scandinavian loans in English may serve to negate Sawyer's claims that, "[u]nfortunately, this linguistic argument for the density of the Scandinavian settlement has only been stated in very general terms and it certainly merits detailed examination" (Sawyer 1969: 169).

This study is of a linguistic nature. But some socio-historical conclusions are also possible, and here both perspectives have been adopted. The use of history as a primary source (chronicles) does not imply any kind of methodology, but constitutes a mere narration of events, and is not always necessarily objective. On the contrary, secondary sources, that is, historiographical works, involve the use of a methodology on the part of the historian as well as an interpretation of the historical events contained in chronicles themselves. Such a methodology is essential in order to carry out any sort of scientific assessment[1]. This socio-historical approach is the reason why Chapter One is devoted to the reconstruction or recreation of the historical events in the transition from the Old English to the Middle English period that lead to the situation analysed in the following chapter.

Chapter Two is devoted to a detailed study of the social and economic organisation of England with special reference to that of the Danelaw in the Old English period. Both historical and social aspects are of paramount importance here for the understanding of lexical transfer from one speech community to another and thus the enlargement and enrichment of available vocabulary. Chapters One and Two, then, are in some way indebted to Ferguson's

---

1 A clear explanation of the opposition between the concepts of chronicle and history is proposed by Collingwood (1946) Collingwood, Dray & Van der Dussen (2001).

(1959: 340) criticism of descriptive approaches such as those of Erik Bjørkman (1900-1912) and Mary Serjeantson (1935) who, as a consequence of their interest in English internal structure, ignored fundamental data on the socio-cultural context in which language exists. It should be also noted that discussions of lexical transfer among linguistic systems have usually been conducted (Clyne 1987: 454) through the presentation of lists of items grouped by topic or, as Bjørkman (1900-1902) himself does, as a mere succession in chronological order.

The difference in the number of terms collected by Erik Bjørkman and the ones I have considered here was evident from the very beginning, and was one of the factors that motivated this study. The aim was to compare these two different counts in some detail and to explore exactly the nature of this difference. My own analysis yields almost 50% more items than Bjørkman's, and while I do not disregard the chronological arrangement that he proposed at the beginning of the twentieth century, I have added a new classification. In addition to classifying terms according to the traditionally accepted linguistic periods of English, then, I have also tried to establish a date for an item's first occurrence in English, using an estimated margin of error of ca. 25 years.[2]

Following Bjørkman, most studies dealing with the presence of Scandinavian elements in English have been of a quantitative nature. Intuition has often been the basis for judgements regarding the sort of North Germanic origin words that are part of the English lexicon. No specific methodology or theoretical framework seems to have been used. For this reason I have framed my own study not only in quantitative terms (that is, the number of Scandinavian terms) but in such a way that I can also address the issues qualitatively (what kind of words were borrowed, looking at grammatical and dialectal variables and, above all, at their distribution in the lexicon). I believe that in this way the use of other variables for the analysis of the items in the data will provide more reliable conclusions than the use of chronology alone.

I have used the following variables: lexical category, assessing the proportion of loanwords for each category; dialect, asking in what areas of the territory the most frequently used Scandinavian loanwords occur, whether

---

[2] All the information referring to word chronology has been extracted from the *Middle English Dictionary*, as will be seen in Chapter Four.

they are restricted to the Danelaw or not, etc.; chronology, considering from what moment we should consider the use of a word to be effective in English; and lexical distribution, addressing the question of which lexical fields show the greatest abundance of Scandinavian terms, in order to ascertain which are the fields that are more directly affected. One of my particular interests here is to see whether Scandinavian vocabulary was restricted to the specific lexical fields of everyday life or if, due to the extent to which they were used by speakers in general, they could be adscribed to the common core of the language. The findings of the analysis, it is hoped, will provide a broader overview than those offered in the last few years.

I have also resorted to sociolinguistics, more specifically, to an approach using the framework of variation studies. For this reason Chapter Three contains a brief account of some of the more relevant models within variation studies, as well as laying out reasons for the application of variation frameworks to the particular case under study here.

Many different possible approaches to analysis have arisen through the influence of sociolinguistics, and my choice will reflect what I consider to be their potential application to many different language situations as well as their scientific rigour. The models that I will consider are those proposed by Labov (1966, 1972, 1984), the social-network model of Lesley and James Milroy (1980, 1990, 1992), and Bailey's (1973, 1987) dynamic model. I will try to ascertain which of these is most appropriate for the study of linguistic processes occurring in historical contexts. Field studies, of course, are not possible for past stages of languages, and the limitations of working diachronically will itself suggest the appropriateness of one model over another, or perhaps the use of an eclectic framework. Other models, those not suitable for the study of the history of English, have not been discussed.

Chapter Four concentrates on a description of the methodology used in the compilation of data for the corpus used in the study. This corpus is, ultimately, derived from written evidence produced in both late Old English and Middle English. I am conscious that the traditional view holds that Scandinavian loanwords are introduced in Middle English, but some authors (Moskowich 1995a, 1995b, 2005a; Moskowich and Seoane 1996; Townend 2006) consider that since Old Norse was not a written language (other than on some runic inscriptions) yet must have been both widely used and long-lasting, perhaps it was already in use and having some effect during the Old English period, and that it was not until Middle English that words of Scandinavian origin came to inhabit English texts, almost at the same time as French loans. Those Scandinavian lexical items appearing in writing from the twelfth century onwards must have arrived in English earlier, since they are sometimes archaic, in the sense that they have not undergone the morphological and phonological changes affecting Old Norse in Scandinavia at the time. Such fossilised Scandinavian forms must, then, have been in use in speech, to be used in writing later on. These terms, belonging to the oral register, would have been adopted in texts only when English rather than Latin was preferred, and this was not until Alfred the Great promoted the use of the vernacular over Latin.[3]

Romaine (1982), discussing methodology, states that contemporary writings are the only materials to be used in research when both sociolinguistics and diachrony are at stake. I take as a basic assumption the claims of Labov and others that language change originates in speech. However, written texts can also be used as evidence of the surprising way that, in the early stages of the language, lexical change occurred first in speech and later in writing. When resorting to written sources I have not limited the sampling of materials to literary works but have included other text types and genres in order to ascertain whether Scandinavian loans are restricted to the years immediately following its appearance in Danelaw English and are used by low-rank social groups, as has been often assumed, or whether these loans are also present in the speech of the ruling classes and in other geographical areas. In fact, in line with Romaine (1982), the difference to be observed between speech and writing may be to some extent comparable to the speech of any individual when he or she is being observed (as in the case of sociolinguistic questionnaires and interviews) and when not. In both cases samples should be considered either valid or not for the study of language on the same grounds.

Throughout this book, and particularly in Chapter Six, I will try to provide conclusions that argue against the traditional view as to the role of North Germanic varieties in English. Hence I will argue, and if possible prove, that

---

[3] Most of the texts in which we have found Scandinavian loans are in fact later texts. Latin was still in use for other purposes until the end of the fourteenth century (Taavitsainen & Pahta 2004).

Anglo-Scandinavian[4] (as I will call it) was not exclusive of the inhabitants of the Danelaw but was more widespread than traditionally believed. Its use should not be regarded as widespread only from a dialectal perspective but also from a diastratic one, in the sense that loanwords were not limited to the lowest social groups but were vertically distributed. In fact, there may be a close relation between geographical and social extension: Scandinavian terms seem to have been well rooted in the common core vocabulary of English and thus would have been accessible to a large number of speakers of different social rank. This same reason accounts for the fact that many originally Scandinavian terms have come down to us in the works of writers and scribes who were both socially and geographically alien to the Danelaw, and hence their use of such terms was probably unconscious.

Notwithstanding this, and considering that there are both internal and external motivations for change (Vann 2009: 177), we should not forget that the speech community responsible for this linguistic change in England from the tenth century onwards was probably a mixed rural one in which Anglo-Saxons and Scandinavians co-existed, and that the socio-cultural level of speakers is a factor determining variation (Samper 2006). In Milroyan terms it is a multiplex community in which most speakers are competent in the colloquial or low variety of both languages whereas only a few are also competent in the corresponding high varieties. In Sánchez-Carrión's (1987) terms they are natural semi-bilingual speakers. It is from this type of community that linguistic change spreads to a point where certain lexical items originally marked as foreign became unmarked and commonly used. This phenomenon would not have been possible without the existence of social networks with dense relationships[5] (and we can consider that a long period of co-existence increases density) since a greater density implies a greater pressure on individual speakers to maintain their own linguistic habits. It could be argued that the density of social relations among members of mixed communities, such as the ones I propose here as the origin of lexical change, was low even though they were small, rural settlements.

---

4   I am using this term as a parallel to Anglo-Norman (Czerniak 2011). Fisiak (1977: 249) already uses the term "Anglo-Norse".

5   The degree of density of networks is related to the number of relationships among the members of that network. When two members of a network establish relations in different contexts the density of the network increases.

Once the sociocultural space for language contact (Watts 2011: 11) has been examined, I will deal with another aspect of language change in passing, that of the loss of inflections and its relation with the contact situation. The diversity of explanations and approaches to the topic may imply that the question has not yet been solved definitely. In fact, two main viewpoints have generally been adopted regarding this issue. One of these claims that the loss of endings in English is due to the dynamics of English itself, scholars tending to base their arguments on phonological criteria (mainly referring to the evolution of non-stressed vowels into schwa and from there to their complete collapse). The second trend relies on more than intra-systemic causes, taking into account the language social context but only in a superficial way, and without providing specific reasons. Most authors within this group consider that it is the Norman Conquest and not the Scandinavian migrations (Stafford 2009) that is most relevant for morphological change. My own position will take both intra- and extra-linguistic events into consideration but, contrary to other more traditional perspectives, will posit that it is in the Scandinavian presence that the dramatic morphological change observed from the beginning to the end of Middle English finds its origins.

Throughout the present work linguistic change and socio-historical events will be revealed as interacting in such a way that it is very difficult to understand one independently from the others.

Chapter One

The historical context

1. Some preliminary considerations

Many studies looking at the presence of the Scandinavians in England have been biased, sometimes too categorical in their claims, and were based on chronicles. Claims were often made without any detailed evidence to support them, as is the case with Geipel (1971: 57) where he claims that "[t]he Norse language was spoken in various parts of the British Isles for a thousand years and more, of this there can be no doubt". However, other studies, not necessarily within the field of medieval history (Jesch 2001a; Moskowich and Crespo 2007), have tried to provide well-grounded information about what the long coexistence of Anglo-Saxons and Scandinavians might have implied.

One of the historical events of paramount importance is the massive movement of Norse speakers from Northern Europe to the British Isles. This movement is said to have taken place in two distinct phases, known as the First and Second Migration, following Cameron (1969), Lund (1969) and Lyons (1977). Dealing with the issues in terms of migration led to divergent opinions. Here we might mention Jesch (2001b) or, before her, Arngart (1947: 73), who noted the large number of Norse female names appearing in twelfth-century Danelaw documents, and commenting on the significance of this: "For they also form a material addition to the evidence, which suggests that something like a genuine migration may have taken place in the ninth century, that, in particular, the armies may have sent for their womenkind when they turned from war to agriculture."

Bjørkman (1910), on the contrary, claims that there were no women among the invaders and that those names found belonged to women of Norse descent on the mothers' side. He points out that, once they had settled as farmers, the Norse ex-soldiers tended to marry native Anglo-Saxon women.

The revision of historical events and contexts is necessary for the understanding of a situation that early authors like William Caxton (in Fernández 1982: 508) already perceived. To his well-known "Loo, what sholde a man in thyse dayes now wryte, egges or eyren?" we could add the words of John of Trevisa:

Al þe longage of þe Norþhumbres, and specialych at ʒork, ys so scharp, slyttyng, and frotyng, and vnschape, þat we souþeron men may þat longage vnneþe vndurstonde. Y trowe þat þat ys bycause þat a buþ nyʒ to strange men and aliens, þat spekeþ strangelych, and also bycause þat þe kynges of Engelond woneþ alwey fer fram þat contray. (In Emerson 1905: 133-134)[6]

John of Trevisa describes the very peculiar historical and political conditions in Northumbria, with a population considered "foreign".

All this is directly related to the research presented here, in that it is evident that sociolinguistic approaches must never ignore the social structure or the historical circumstances of the community under study. Scandinavian writers also refer to the special linguistic situation of England in the Middle Ages. Thus, in *Gunnlaugs Saga Ormstungu* we are told how the main character, Gunnlaug, travels to England with another traveller to try his luck as a "skald" (court poet). What happens to him during his journey, at a moment in which both cultural and material exchanges were frequent, is reflected below:

> Þá réð fyrir Englandi Aðalráðr konungr Játgeirsson, ok var góðr hofðingi. Hann sat þenna vetr í Lundúnaborg. Ein var þá tunga á Englandi sem í Nóregi ok í Danmorku, en þá skiptusk tungur í Englandi, er Vilhjálmr bastarðr varr England. Gekk þaðan af í Englandi valska, er hann var þaðan ættaðr.[7]

If we accept this claim, we could assume that the reasons for such similarities are not only linguistic and due to genealogical factors, but that historical and social elements also play a paramount role. Therefore, we could accept Serjeantson's hypothesis (1935: 61):

> The Scandinavian element in English is due in the first place to the Viking invasions of England in the 8th, 9th and 11th centuries, and their forcible settlement

---

6   "All the language of the Northumbrians, and especially at York, is so sharp, piercing, rasping, and amorphous, that we Southeners can hardly understand it. I reckon that this is because they are near outlandish men and foreigners, who speak in foreign tongues, and also because the kings of England always live far from that area". (Tr. by B. Cottle 1969).

7   "At that time there ruled over England King Ethelred, son of Edgar, and he was a good prince. He was passing his winter in London. At that time there was the same speech in England as in Norway and Denmark, but the speech in England was changed when William the Bastard won the land. French prevailed in England from that time forth, since he himself was French by birth." (Tr. by Ashdown 1930: 190-191).

in parts of the country, but also, and in much greater degree, to the peaceful association of Englishman and Scandinavian during the 11th and 12th centuries...

According to Serjeantson, this association provoked the following situation: "For some time the Danes must have been bilingual, and no doubt many of their English neighbours and fellow-villagers and townsmen learnt to speak Danish" (Serjeantson 1935: 62).

The same idea is reinforced some years later by other scholars. Arngart (1947: 76) claims that "[t]he numerous Scandinavian loan-words in English would also hardly be accounted for without the assumption that individuals of English nationality (or English-speaking individuals of Scandinavian descent) endeavoured to acquire the Scandinavian language."

Lockwood (1975) argues in favour of the existence of Anglo-Scandinavian. It may certainly be more reasonable to think that there existed some linguistic situation by which neither the Anglo-Saxons learnt Old Norse nor the Scandinavians learnt Old English, but rather that both resorted to a mixed code originating in communicative needs and social pressure. In Lockwood's words (1975: 203): "It seems likely that over wide areas a compromise colloquial arose, a Scandinavian-English dialect which concentrated on basic comprehension, without undue regard for grammatical niceties."

Before proceeding any further, the factors bringing about this linguistic situation must be considered in some detail.

2. Causes for the Scandinavian expansion

When dealing with the presence of the Scandinavians in England, their reasons for moving throughout the continent and even beyond are often given scant discussion, since it has generally been often taken for granted that the principal motivation was little more than pillaging and raiding. However, some authors have tried to go beyond the information provided by medieval English chronicles and discover exactly what compelled these northern tribes to leave their homeland for other unknown places in the first place. Among others, Geipel (1971: 31) offers some clues for this massive movement:

> Famine, pestilence, cataclysmic natural disasters in their native land, overpopulation as a result of the widespread practice of polygamy, the custom of driving out younger sons to fend for themselves, the cutting off by the Arabs of the old trade connections with Byzantium, an obsessive mania to destroy other people's prop-

erty, a fanatical loathing of Christianity, and an insatiable appetite for high adventure – these and many other suggestions have been put forward as likely explanations for the prodigious outboiling of people from the north that is part of the conventional concept of the 'Viking eruption'.

Even if any of these factors might have constituted a motive for a particular tribe or clan to move, we should not consider them as the cause for the whole phenomenon that lasted over 250 years, the so-called Viking Age. In Geipel's words (1971: 30):

> [...] although it is impossible to pinpoint the precise moment when 'proto-Vikings' became Vikings proper, most Scandinavian historians define what they call Vikingetiden -the Viking Age- as the 250 years between AD 800 and 1050, the era of the long-range peregrinations that carried men of Danish, Swedish and Norwegian birth as far as Baghdad, Byzantium and Labrador.

The counterpart to this idea can be found in Graham-Campbell and Kidd (1980: 20) when they affirm that "The idea that the Vikings suddenly emerged as a phenomenon peculiar to the 9th, 10th and 11th centuries is a misconception based on their sudden explosion into the consciousness of Western Europe". Taking into account what we know about Europe in the Middle Ages this seems to be the most likely situation. According to Geipel, there may have been cases of over-population related to the practice of polygamy in some geographical areas in Scandinavia and Jutland. Likewise, it is also true that life conditions were hard but "the traditional concept of an excessively fecund, volatile, rain-sodden population bursting at the seams and then erupting outwards in all directions —and continuing to erupt for 250 years— is nowadays critically regarded as reflecting too literal an interpretation of the early records" (1971: 31).

Another cause for this expansion mentioned by Geipel is the fact that, as farmers of little productive soil,[8] the Scandinavians tried to find new places with better conditions in which to settle, which they simply took if these could not be obtained by means of commercial exchanges (Moskowich and Crespo 2007). If the Norsemen reached further than the rest of the inhabitants

---

8   Ploughing and farming must have been very difficult if we consider statements such as the following: "Scandinavia was inhabited by farmers where the land was productive. Farms were often single units worked by family groups, clustering more densely where the land was best. Farming was supplemented by hunting and fishing where possible" (Graham-Campbell & Kidd 1980: 20).

of Europe in the period it was not because they were more violent than other peoples but because of their technological superiority as sailors. My contention is that this phenomenon involves all of Europe. Both Danes and Norwegians had been traders for generations, and indeed it was through trade that they came in contact with Southern and Western civilisations and with places where they saw fertile lands and Christian monasteries containing more riches than they could ever have imagined.

In 854 the royal dynasty disappeared in Denmark. With it, the figure of a powerful king faded and, together with the generally poor conditions, it was inevitable that warrior chieftains and noblemen would disperse towards other territories. Thus from around 850 some of the men formerly depending on the king went raiding southwards.

For generations, Scandinavian tradesmen had had two main commercial routes depending on whether they were Norsemen or Danes: the former circumnavigated the North of Scotland to the Western Isles and to the South; the latter approached the Eastern and Southern coasts of England and France. Hence, following these routes, it can be inferred that raids and settlements in Ireland, Scotland, Wales and Cornwall were basically by Norwegians whereas those coming from England and France were by Danes (Sawyer 1982). Notwithstanding this, we know that contemporary Anglo-Saxon chroniclers use the terms "heathen", "pirates" or "Danes" to refer to the different ethnic groups: "Early chroniclers seldom troubled to discriminate between Norwegian, Swedish and Danish Vikings, and all northern marauders were liable to be dubbed 'Danes' as, for example, were the Norwegians who had axed Beaduheard at Portland in 787" (Geipel 1971: 34).

To understand the reasons why the Danes were thus pushed towards England it is also necessary to take into account the increasingly frequent conflicts they had with the Franks from the early ninth century. Charlemagne and his heirs had not only interrupted the Scandinavian commercial route with Byzantium and the Middle East, but they had also commenced upon an expansive policy which was encroaching on Danish territory. The Obodrites[9], originally Slavic vassals of the Carolingian Empire, crossed the borderline of

---

9   The confederation of West Slavic tribes known as the Obodrites had been taken to settle the Eastern area of Holstein and Mecklenburg, previously inhabitted by the Saxons but annihilated by Charlemagne.

the Danevirke – a defensive earth ditch separating Jutland from the continent built by King Godfred – and invaded Danish territory.

These conflicts did not stop when Charlemagne died. His son Louis succeeded him in 814, inheriting a perfectly fortified Empire. And Louis clashed with the Danes again when he backed Harald Klak, pretender to the Danish throne, though not the legitimate heir. From Frisia, Harald Klak managed to get to Jutland but King Godgred's legitimate heirs resisted in the Northern Isles thanks to their superiority as seafarers. Using these Isles as their base, they began raiding the areas of Holstein and Mecklenburg.

Later on, when in the early 830s Louis' sons fought their father, the Isles Danes (now forced to become Vikings) took advantage of the weakened imperial defences. When Louis died, the Empire was divided among his sons and finally collapsed.

> From now on, Danish Vikings harried annually down the coasts of the three kingdoms, from the Elbe to the Garonne, pillaging such important trade centres as Rouen, Nantes and Quentovic, and making occasional lightning raids across the Channel to the south coast of England. (Geipel 1971: 39)

In contrast to what happened in other societies, the Vikings were not obliged to serve the same lord for their entire lives, but could choose who they wanted to fight for and in this sense were mercenaries, only temporarily associated with their lords. As Whitelock (1955: 29) notes, "…loyalty is personal, not tribal, for a successful chief may attract to him men from many tribes." Thus, European history has been witness on occasion to Scandinavians fighting other Scandinavians, when at a particular moment they were allied to a lord who was engaged in a conflict with their fellow countrymen. It is this same relatively free condition that allows them to settle on the continent as warriors serving some chieftain or king and from there, mainly from the Rhine, to travel to England:

> The Danes who had been granted land hereabouts by the emperor Louis and his son Lothar, in return for their aid in repelling others of their species, had rapidly reverted to type, and it was probably these Frisian-based Vikings who were responsible for the series of stabbing raids along the south coast of England from Sheppey to Cornwall that punctuated the 830s. (Geipel 1971: 38)

The Norsemen who settled in the North Atlantic Islands and Ireland were defeated by the natives several times in the first half of the ninth century. This conflict encouraged the Danes to move westwards. The arrival of the Danes in Ireland provoked a phenomenon that is not observed in England: the inhabitants of Ireland made a distinction between Norsemen and Danes, which was not the case of England, as can be inferred from the chronicles. Such a situation is perfectly illustrated by Geipel (1971: 39), when he says: "Vicious fighting broke out immediately between the newcomers – called by the Irish 'Black Strangers', perhaps on account of the colour they painted their shields – and the 'White Strangers', or Norwegians, still in Ireland."

3. The Scandinavians in England: the Danelaw

Archaeological evidence (Hines 1984) showed that a cultural relation between the British Isles and Scandinavia had existed in both directions from ancient times. Apparently, these relations were taking place long before the British Isles split completely from the continent during the Neolithic and the Bronze Age (Geipel 1971: 28-ff). As far as cultural intercourse is concerned, legends and myths with shared features testify both to common origin and close exchange. As claimed by Geipel (1971: 29), all these contacts took place before the eighth century:

> It was not only in their language that the Angles and other Jutland expatriates in England retained their connection with their ancestral homeland. Their traditions — as recorded in *Beowulf, Widsith* and the *Finnesburh Fragment* — kept fresh for many generations the memory of their legendary heroes and their former intimate association with the Scandinavian world, an association that was eventually to be renewed by the coming of the longships to Britain.

Although such contacts had existed for a long time, the first recorded evidence we have regarding the arrival of the Scandinavians into England is an isolated mention from 787[10], with which we could consider the Viking Age to

---

10   Besides Smith's (1935) classical edition of the *Parker Chronicle*, I have resorted to the one by Garmonsway (1953). This author classifies the different extant manuscripts in the following way: Manuscript A (*The Parker Chronicle*), Corpus Christi College, Cambridge, MS. 173, folios 1-32 [60 a.C. – 1070 d.C.], Manuscripts B and C (*The Abingdon Chronicle*) divided so that Manuscript B corresponds to British Museum, Cotton MS. Tiberius A vi, folios 1-34; [1 d.C.-977 d.C.] and Manuscript C to British Museum, Cotton MS. Tiberius B i, folios 115-64; [60 a.C.-1066 d.C.]; Manuscript D (*The Worcester Chronicle*), British Museum, Cotton MS. Tiberius B

have begun in England. Indeed, Janzén (1972: 1) opens his study of the subject in the following way:

> The first time we hear about Viking expeditions to the West is 787, by Norwegians, at which time Norwegian Viking fleets attacked several places along Ireland's coast, originating from the Hebrides and other islands north of Scotland where Norwegian colonies had then already been established.

And Garmonsway's (1953: 54) edition of the *Chronicle* contains the following for the record corresponding to that year:

> Anno dcclxxxvii. Her nom Beorhtric cyning Offan dohtor Eadburge. & on his dagum cuomon ærest iii. scipu. & þa se gerefa þær to rad. & hie wolde drifan to þæs cyninges tune. þy he nyste hwæt hie wæron. & hiene mon ofslog. Dæt wæron þa ærestan scipu Deniscra monna þe Angelcynnes lond gesohton.[11]

This quotation, as well as the two that follow, make reference to the first misdeeds of the men from Northern Europe in England. Although, as stated above, the term "Dane" is often used to refer to the Scandinavians in general and not to people of Danish descent, these early incursions were almost exclusively carried out by Norwegians. In the last decades of the eighth century many Norwegian farmers (*hænder*) had settled with their families in the Northern Islands, in the Orkneys and Shetland, bringing their language and institutions with them. They were also assimilated by the native population (Geipel 1971: 34). The description in the *Chronicle* seems to pay no special attention to the fact that they are Scandinavian but instead to the apparent violence of the event:

---

iv: [1 d.C.-1079 d.C., to which an annal for 1080 (=1130) is added]; Manuscript E (*The Laud (Peterborough) Chronicle*), Bodleian MS. Laud 636: 1 d.C.-1153 d.C.]; Manuscript F (*The Bilingual Canterbury Epitome*), British Museum, Cotton MS. Domitian A viii: [1 d.C.-1058 d.C.]. This is the classification I will use when quoting. If not otherwise stated, I will be referring to the *Parker Chronicle*.

11 "In this year king Beorhtric took to wife Eadburh, daughter of Offa. And in his days came for the first time three ships: and then the reeve rode thither and tried to compel them to go to the royal manor, for he did not know what they were, and they slew him. These were the first ships of Danes to come to England."

Anno dcclxxxvii. Her Brihtric cing nam Offan dohter Eadburhge to wiue. & on his dagan coman ærost III. scipa Norðmanna of Hereða lande. Ðæt wæran þa ærostan scipa Deniscra manna ðe Angelcynnes land gesohton.[12]

Anno dcclxxxvii. Her nam Breohtric cining Offan dohter Eadburge. & on his dagum comon ærest Ill. scipu Norðmanna of Hereðalande. & þa se gerefa þær to rad. & hi wolde drifan to þes cininges tune. þy he nyste hwæt hi wæron. & hine man ofsloh þa. Ðæt w æron þa erestan scipu Deniscra manna þe Angelcynnes land gesohton.[13]

The next reference to the Scandinavians is found in *Laud Chronicle* and corresponds to the entry for 794 (Garmonsway 1953: 57):

...And Northumbria was ravaged by the heathen, and Ecgfrith's monastery at Donemup [Jarrow] looted; and there one of their leaders was slain, and some of their ships besides were shattered by storms: and many of them were drowned there, and some came ashore alive and were at once slain at the river mouth.

The *Parker Chronicle* offers more information on the successive arrivals of Scandinavians to England in an entry for 832 (which really corresponds to 835, as explained by Smith 1935: 9-12)[14]. The entries for the following years also mention the "Danes":

---

12 Fragment from *The Bilingual Canterbury Epitome* (Manuscript F) in Thorpe 1861. "In this year king Beorhtric took to wife Eadburh, daughter of king Offa; and in his days came for the first time three ships of Norwegians from Hörthaland [around Hardanger Fjord]: these were the first ships of the Danes to come to England." (Tr. Garmonsway 1953: 54).

13 From Manuscript E (*The Laud (Peterborough) Chronicle*) (Thorpe 1861). "In this year Beorhtric took to wife Eadburh, daughter of king Offa. And in his days came first three ships of Norwegians from Hörthaland [around Hardanger Fjord]: and then the reeve rode thither and tried to compel them to go to the royal manor, for he did not know what they were: and then they slew him. These were the first ships of the Danes to come to England". (Tr. Garmonsway 1953: 55).

14 The lack of coincidence in chronological information, in the sense that certain events may be recorded one, two or even three years before expected, is explained by Beaven (1918). The year in which events were recorded depended on the date system used, that is, on the year in which the chronicler started his counting. In the Middle Ages several calendars co-existed so that the year could begin on: (1) The Annunciation (March 25th) preceding January 1st (called "stylus Pisanus"); (2) September 1st, preceding January 1st (Constantinople's Indiction); (3) September 24th, preceding January 1st (Caesarean Indiction); (4) December 25th preceding January

Anno dcccxxxii. Her hæþne men oferhereadon Sceapiʒe.[15]

Anno dcccxxxiii. Her ʒefeaht Ecʒbryht cyning wiþ xxxu sciphlæsta æt Carrum & ðær wearþ micel wæl ʒeslæʒen, & þa Denescan ahton wælstowe ʒewald; & Hereferþ & Wiʒþen tueʒen biscepas forþferdon, & Dudda & Osmod tueʒen aldormen forþferdon.[16]

Anno dcccxxxu. Her cuom micel sciphere on West-Walas & hie to anum ʒecierdon, & wiþ Ecʒbryht West Seaxna cyning winnende wæron. Ða he þæt hierde & mid fierde ferde & him wiþ feaht aet Heʒestdune & þær ʒefliemde ʒe þa Walas ʒe þa Deniscan.[17]

These references to the Scandinavians seem to be quite objective in the sense that the chronicler is not setting out to judge them. In Morgan's words (1989: 91) "The Viking landing was a minor affair". This neutral perspective may be accounted for by the fact that the Anglo-Saxons were used to continuous wars among their different kingdoms as well as to treat and sometimes abuse the Celts inhabiting the territories that lay before them. This meant that violent behaviour was normal and would not surprise them. Besides this, they did not have the feeling of belonging to a political unit in the sense that we do today: sharing the land would have been habitual.

The Vikings were active during one of the most restless periods in recorded history; large-scale tribal movements and ethnic displacements were the order of the day, and it was only their superior seamanship that distinguished the Scandinavians from all the other footloose and land-hungry peoples who swilled about Europe at this time. (Geipel 1971: 32)

1st, and (6) on The Annunciation (March 25th) following January 1st ("stylus Florentinus"). Cf. Garmonsway 1953: Intr. XIX-XXX.

15   "In this year the heathen devastated Sheppey". Tr. Garmonsway (1953: 62).
16   "In this year king Egbert fought against thirty-five ships' companies at Carhampton; and great slaughter was made there, and the Danes had possession of the place of slaughter. And Herefrith and Wigthegn, two bishops, passed away; and Dudda and Osmod, two ealdormen, passed away". Tr. Garmonsway (1953: 62).
17   "In this year came a great pirate host to Cornwall, and they [the Danes and the Britons of Cornwall] united, and continued fighting against Egbert, king of Wessex. Then he heard this and proceeded with his levies and fought against them at Hingston Down, and there put to fight both Britons and Danes". Tr. Garmonsway (1953: 62).

All that we know from what we are told in the entry for 836 (833, according to Smith) is that thirty-five ships arrive on English soil[18], which probably implies between seven hundred and one thousand men. The first confrontation seems to have taken place in 837 (probably 840):

> Anno dcccxxxuii. Her Wulfheard aldormon ʒefeaht æt Hamtune wiþ xxxiii sciphlæsta & þær micel wæl ʒesloʒ & siʒe nom. & þy ʒeare forþferde Wulfheard. & þy ilcan ʒeare ʒefeaht Æþelhelm dux wiþ Deniscne here on Port mid Dornsætum & ʒode hwile þone here ʒefliemde, & þa Deniscan ahton wælstowe ʒewald & wone aldormon ofsloʒon.[19]

From this entry onwards, *here* is the term generally used to refer to the Scandinavians. Already in Ine's Law (King of Wessex, 688-726), references to groups of men between seven and thirty-five are called *hloþ*, whereas the term *here* always implies more than thirty-five men. It is clear, then, that all following references to the Scandinavians imply a growing number of men. The greater the number of men, the more negative the comments are. In this way, the entry for 840 (last mention of Deniscan until 845[20]) is as follows:

> Anno dcccxl. Her Æþelwulf cyninʒ ʒefeaht æt Carrum wiþ xxxu sciphlæsta, & þa Deniscan ahton wælstowe ʒewald.[21]

As the tone of the narration changes, a new phenomenon typical of the period now emerges. In the entry corresponding to 865 in the *Parker Chronicle,* we

---

18   It should be noticed that chronicles refer to the ships as a means of providing information on the number of men on board. According to the findings of Gokstad and Oseberg (Norway), the ships of the Viking Age are between twenty-two and twenty-four metres long and five wide. They have sixteen holes where oars were placed. With all the oars out the crew could be formed by thirty or thirty-three men. Later, better and lighter ships were discovered in Roskilde. These could transport up to one hundred warriors. Among the long ships, the one known as Trondheim's Long Serpent, ca. 1000, was thirty-seven metres long and could shelter 200 men aboard (Cohat 1989; Atkinson 1990).
19   Smith (1935) claims that the apparent contradiction here is due to the fact that the ealdormen could stop the Scandinavians for some time but the latter finally won.
20   From 840 to 845 the Danes moved all over the continent. This may explain the absence of information about them in the Anglo-Saxon chronicles.
21   "[843]. In this year king Æthelwulf fought at Carhampton against thirty-five ships' companies, and the Danes had possession of the place of slaughter." Tr. Garmonsway (1953: 64).

find the word *danegeld* for the first time. The *danegeld*[22] is somehow a form of tax that would last for several centuries, though with the nature and means of payment varying considerably:

> Anno dccclxu. Her sæt hæþen here on Tenet & ӡenamon friþ wiþ Cantþarum, & Cantþare him feoh ӡeheton wiþ þam friþe, & under þam friþe & þam feohӡehate se here hiene on niht up bestæl, & oferherӡeade alle Cent eastewearde.

The *micel here* is first mentioned in 866. This fact has led to many different approaches and controversies regarding the possibility or impossibility of the settlers in Britain being only soldiers. The idea of a general migration, once proposed by Cameron (1969: 177) in the light of the evidence of place-names, is today widely accepted.

> Anno dccclxui. Her fenӡ Æþered Æþelbryhtes broþur to Wesseaxna rice; & þy ilcan ӡeare cuom micel here on Angelcynnes lond & wintersetl namon on East-Enӡlum & þær ӡehorsude wurdon & hie wiþ him friþ namon.[23]

> Anno dccclxuii. Her for se here of East-Enӡlum ofer Humbre muþan to Eoforwicceastre on Norþymbre, & þær wæs micel unӡeþuærnes þære þeode betweox him selfum, & hie hæfdum hiera cyning aworpenne Osbryht & unӡecyndne cyninӡ underfenӡon Ællan; & hie on ӡeare to þam ӡecirdon, þæt hie wiþ þone here winnende wærun, & hie þeah micle fierd ӡeӡadrodon & þone here sohton æt Eoforwicceastre & on þa ceastre bræcon & hie sume inne wurdon; & þær was unӡemetlic wæ ӡeslæӡen Norþanhymbra, sume binnan, sume butan, & þa cyninӡas beӡen ofslæӡenӡ, & sio laf wiþ þone here friþ nam. & þy ilcan ӡeare ӡefor Ealchstan biscep & he hæfde þæt bisceprice l wintra æt Scireburnan, & his lic liþ þær on tune.[24]

---

22 The first element in this compound reinforces the idea that all Scandinavians were considered Danes by the Anglo-Saxons. Today we know many of the raiders were Norwegians or Swedes (Wainwright 1947: 96-119).

23 "In this year Æthelred, brother of Æthelbert, succeeded to the kingdom of Wessex. And this same year came a great host to England and took winter-quarters in East-Anglia, and there were provided with horses, and they made peace with them." Tr. Garmonsway (1953: 68).

24 "In this year the host went from East Anglia over the mouth of the Humber to York in Northumbria; and there was great dissension of the people among themselves; and they had repudiated their king Osberht and accepted Ælla, a king not of royal birth; and it was late in the year when they set about making war against the host, nevertheless they gathered great levies and went to attack the host at York and stormed the city [21 March 867], and some of them got inside; and immense slaughter was

The army was led by Ragnar Lothbrok's sons[25]. It seems (Smith 1935: 24) that the army reached Britain in the autumn of 865 and settled in Northumbria (876), Mercia (877) and East Anglia (880):

> Anno dccclxuiii. Her for se ilca here innan Mierce to Snotenʒaham & þær wintersetl namon. & Burʒræd Miercna cyning & his wiotan bædon Æþered West-Seaxna cyning & Ælfred his broþur þæt hie him ʒefultumadon, þæt hie wiþ þone here ʒefuhton; & þa ferdon hie mid Wesseaxna fierde innan Mierce oþ Snotenʒaham & þone here þær metton on þam ʒeweorce, & þær nan hefelic ʒefeoht ne wearþ, & Mierce friþ namon wiþ þone here.[26]

The above description is the first to be found in the regular recording of the movements of this army across Britain. The chronicles regularly detail the atrocities of these heathen peoples, starting with the East-Anglian King Edmund's martyrdom when he refused to become Ingvar's vassal:

> Anno dccclxx. Her rad se here ofer Mierce innan East-Enʒle & wintersetl namon æ Weodforda. & þy wintre Eadmund cyning him wiþ feaht & þa Deniscan siʒe namon & þone cyning ofsloʒon & þæt lond all ʒeeodon.[27] & þy ʒeare ʒefor Ceol-

---

 made of the Northumbrians there, some inside, some outside, and both the kings were slain, and the remnant made peace with the host. And in the same year died bishop Ealhstan, and he held the episcopal see at Sherborne fifty years; and his body lies there in the churchyard." Tr. Garmonsway (1953: 68).

25 Both the legend and the *Saga of Ragnar Lothbrok* coincide in indicating that the reason for Ragnar's son's trip to Northumbria is revenge on their father's death, murderd by Ælla. This trip provokes the fall of York, which was afterwards in Scandinavian hands for a long period.

26 "In this year the same host went into Mercia to Nottingham, and there took winter-quarters. And Burhred, king of Mercia, and his councillors begged Æthelred, king of Wessex, and his brother Alfred to help them fight against the host; and then they proceeded with the West Saxon levies into Mercia as far as Nottingham, and there came upon the host in the fortification, but there was no serious engagement, and the Mercians made peace with the host." Tr. Garmonsway (1953: 70).

27 Although Garmonsway translates this fragment as stated in the following footnote, so that ʒeeodon means "overrun", I think this verb may be interpreted as in Bosworth & Toller, (1898-1921), that is, as one of the acceptions of OE *ge-gan* PE "to occupy". Such an interpretation would reinforce the idea of a colonisation expressed by Cameron, which I share.

noþ ærcebiscep; & Æþered Wiltunscire biscop weraþ ʒecoren to ærcebiscpe to Cantuareberi.²⁸

From this moment onwards several battles are enumerated and their dates are given with great precision. Such is the case of the battles of Reading (28th of December, 870), Englefield (31st of December, 870), Reading again (4th of January, 871), Ashdown (8th of January, 871), Basing (22nd of January, 871) and *Meretune*²⁹ (22nd of March, 871). All these battles share the very well organised opposition of King Ælfred of Wessex, following Æthelred's death.

Successive battles give place to settlements. Garmonsway's translation of "Norþanhymbra lond ʒedælde" as "they shared out the lands of Northumbria" seems to limit the first Scandinavian settlement of which we have any written evidence to Yorkshire (Smith 1935: 30, n. 7), and appears in the entry for the year 876:

> Anno dccclxxui. Her hiene bestæl se here into Werham Wesseaxna fierde & wiþ þone here se cyning friþ nam & him þa aþas sworon on þam halʒan beaʒe, þe hie ær nanre þeode noldon, þæt hie hrædlice of his rice foren; & hie þa under þam hie nihtes bestælon þære fierde, se ʒehorsoda here, into Escanceaster. & þy ʒeare Healfdene Norþanhymbra lond ʒedælde & erʒende wæron & hiera tilʒende.³⁰

Alfred's fortification implied that when Wessex was attacked again in 878 the Scandinavian army had decreased in number since the *micel here* was now divided in two: one part was led by Halfdan, who settled in Yorkshire, and

---

28 "In this year the host rode across Mercia into East Anglia, and took winter-quarters at Thetford; and the same winter king Edmund fought against them, and the Danes won the victory, and they slew the king and overran the entire kingdom. And the same year died archbishop Ceolnoth; and Æthelred, bishop of Wiltshire, was elected archbishop of Canterbury". Tr. Garmonsway (1953: 70).

29 The site of this battle is still disputed, since the placename was quite common in OE (Smith 1935: 27).

30 "[875] In this year the host eluded the West Saxon levies and got into Wareham. And [876] the king made peace with the host, and they swore him oaths on the sacred ring, which before they would never do to any nation, that they would quickly leave this kingdom; and then, under cover of this agreement they evaded the English levies by night, and the mounted host got into Exeter. And in this year Halfdan shared out the lands of Northumbria, and they were engaged in ploughing and in making a living for themselves." Tr. Garmonsway (1953: 74).

the other by Guthrum, Oscytel and Anund[31] and colonised Lincolnshire, Nottinghamshire, Derbyshire and Leicestershire from 877 (Morgan 1989: 93-94). Halfdan soon retired to Ireland because his brother Ivarr, who ruled as "king of all Norsemen in Britain and Ireland", was sacking paleolithic tombs and provoking great tensions among the natives with his behaviour. However, many men belonging to Halfan's army decided not to follow him but to stay in Northumbria and settle as farmers there (Geipel 1971: 41).

In 878, Guthrum's army was defeated by Alfred. The Treaty of Wedmore established the obligation of the defeated to be baptised. In Morgan's (1989: 94) words: "The Danish leader Guthrum accepted baptism with several of his captains, and the two kings settled peace terms". In the *Parker Chronicle* these events are narrated as follows:

> ...& þa salde se here him foreʒislas & micle aþas, þæt hie of his rice uuoldon, & him eac ʒeheton þæt hiera kyninʒ fulwihte onfon wolde & hie þæt ʒelæston swa. & þæs ymb iii wiecan com se cyning to him ʒodrum þritiʒa sum þara monna, þe in þam here weorþuste wæron, æt Alre, & þæt is wiþ Æþelinʒʒaeiʒe; & his se cyning þær onfenʒ æt fulwihte & his crismlisinʒ was æt Weþmor & he was xii niht mid þam cyninge & he hine miclum & his ʒeferan mid feo weorðude.[32]

Most of the army leaves for Ghent before the end of 879. Between then and 885 chroniclers are silent about the Danes even though many of Guthrum's men had decided to stay in Britain and settle as farmers. In 885 we hear about the siege of Rochester, in which an uncertain number of Scandinavians back from France are retained by Alfred:

> Anno dccclxxxu. Her todælde se foresprecena here on tu, oþer dæl east, oþer dæl to Hrofesceastre, & ymbsæton ða ceastre & worhton oþer fæsten ymb hie selfe,

---

31 These names appear in Smith's edition of the *Parker Chronicle* as *Heafdene*, ʒodrum, *Oscytel* and *Anwynd,* respectively. Smith himself recommends Bjørkman (1910, 1912) and Jonsson (1915) for further details.

32 "... and then the host gave him preliminary hostages and solemn oaths that they would leave his kingdom, and promised him in addition that their king would receive baptism; and they fulfilled this promise in the following manner. And three weeks later the king Guthrum came to him, one of thirty of the most honourable men in the host, at Aller which is near Athelney, where the king stood sponsor to him at baptism; and the ceremony of the removal of the baptismal fillet took place at Wedmore, and he was twelve days with the king, who greatly honoured him and his companions with riches." Tr. Garmonsway (1953: 76).

& hie þeah þa ceastre aweredon oþþæt Ælfred com utan mid fierde. Ða eode se here to hiera scipum & forlet þæt ȝeweorc, & hie wurdon þær behorsude, & sone þy ilcan sumere ofer sæ ȝewiton. & þy ilcan ȝeare sende Ælfred cyning sciphere on East-Enȝle. Sona swa hie comon on Sture muþan, þa metton hie xui scipu wicenȝa & wiþ ða ȝefuhton, & þa scipo alle ȝeræhton & þa men ofsloȝon. Ða hie þa hamweard wendon mid þære herehyþe, þa metton hie micelne sciphere wicenȝa & þa wiþ þa ȝefuhton þy ilcan dæȝe, & þa Deniscan ahton siȝe.[33]

According to Blair (1970, 1977) and Morgan (1989: 94) the systematic occupation of the North and East of England by the Danes starts in 880. This would mark the foundation of the Danelaw:

> These [the peace terms] recognized the Danish occupation of much of England as a *fait accompli*. The frontier ran roughly north-westwards from London to Chester; Guthrum was to withdraw with his troops behind his line, where he was to be recognized as king of an independent kingdom. By the autumn of 880 the Danes had left Wessex and begun the systematic settlement of East Anglia.

It is not easy to imagine the extent to which the creation of this independent political unit affected both the Anglo-Saxons and the newcomers. The fact that England did not exist as a political unit makes it easy to understand Arbman and Binns' (1961: 62) assumption that, since England had been previously divided into small kingdoms, internal strife was no novelty and the Danes could be readily accepted.

As for the invaders, we know that King Guthrum was baptised as Athelstan after accepting Alfred's peace conditions, as recorded in the *Parker Chronicle* in the entry for 890. Some of Guthrum's officers were also baptised. Cameron (1965: 3), along with several other writers on the Scandinavian influence on England, defends the idea that it is entirely possible that

---

33   "[884] In this year the above-mentioned host separated into two, one part east and the other part to Rochester, and besieged the city; and they built another fortification around themselves; and the citizens, however, defended the city until Alfred came to their relief [885] with levies. Then went the host to the ships and abandoned the encampment, and were there deprived of their horses, and soon the same summer went oversea. And the same year king Alfred sent a naval force into East Anglia. As soon as they came to the mouth of Stour, then they met sixteen ships of pirates and fought against them, and captured all the ships, and slew the crews. When they were on their way home with the booty, they met a great fleet of pirates, and fought against them the same day, and the Danish were victorious." Tr. Garmonsway (1953: 78).

Scandinavian settlers could have made their homes here, under the protection of the armies of the Five Boroughs during the two generations following 877. These settlers may never have been mentioned in English sources. Other writers, such as Brönsted (1973: 54), consider their settlement in the following terms:

> North of the Thames, as far as Chester, and to the east of a line roughly coinciding with the old Roman Watling Street, was the region occupied and colonized by the Danes and called the Danelaw — comprising parts of Mercia and Deira as well as East Anglia. In these areas the Vikings settled down as farmers, a society of free men with their own laws, customs, and language — the latter still evident in the place-names of this part of the country.

Be this as it may, it seems to be true that the Danes kept certain habits. Morgan (1989: 96) explains that even after the bringing under English rule and Christianisation of the Danelaw it retained striking peculiarities, with its own manorial structure, systems measurement, law, and social differentiation. East Anglia was used as the headquarters for campaigns on the continent, just as they had used the North Atlantic Isles in the past. In this way they continued their actions in Saxony, parts of Germany and, above all, in France.[34] During this period, Alfred continued the fortification of Wessex[35]. Similarly, he created a smaller but more efficient army (Morgan 1989: 95) and urged the construction of a fleet. With all these resources he avoided the expansion of the Danelaw into Wessex.

In 892 there was a new Danish invasion under Hásteinn, another son of Ragnar Lothbrok, whose success was known to all Scandinavians in Britain. As soon as they knew that Hásteinn was approaching, they joined this new wave of Norsemen and abandoned the promise of the peace made with Alfred. The war between Alfred and Hásteinn lasted four years. The Norse troops now moved extremely quickly throughout the South and the Midlands. After several defeats, and seeing that there was no possibility of conquering the land, Hásteinn and his men dispersed, most of them going to Normandy.

---

34 The Siege of Paris lasted one year, from November 885 to November 886.
35 The *Burghal Hidage* provides a complete list of the thirty fortified towns or burghs, one of which was Winchester, whose streets have a strategic design ignoring the previous Roman planification.

The colonists were nowhere extirpated, they seem to have offered scant resistance to the reclamation of their lands, and their absorption into the fabric of the English nation appears to have taken place without undue violence. By 921, following the defeat by Edward of Jórik Guthrumsson, Danish overlord of East Anglia, almost the whole of England was back in native hands. (Geipel 1971: 46-47)

According to the information in the *Parker Chronicle*, 893 was the worst year for struggles between Scandinavians and Anglo-Saxons. The two armies that had originated in the *micel here* were settled in Appledore and Milton Royal, South and North of Kent, respectively. Alfred was thus forced to stand between both, although he in fact managed to make the army in Milton retreat to Essex. The years between 893 and 896 are characterised by the continuous conflicts between Hásteinn and Alfred. From 896 onwards, the Scandinavians went back to East Anglia, Northumbria and France. This constitutes the end of the wars with Alfred:

Anno dcccxcvi.[36] Đa þæs on sumera on ðysum 3ere tofor se here, sum on East-En3le, sum on Norðymbre, & þa þe feohlease wæron him þær scipu begeton & suð ofer sæ foron to Si3ene.[37]

Although many Scandinavians had abandoned English soil, many others had settled there, and the traces they had left by this stage in the Middle Ages are so important that they cannot be ignored.

4. The Second Migration

The hypothesis of the Second Migration posited in the 1970s certainly clashes with the idea that the Norse cultural presence in England is solely due to the group of warriors that, once the *micel here* was defeated, dispersed and settled, mixing with the native population. Likewise, the linguistic repercussions on English are better explained if we accept this migration. Therefore, Lund's (1969, 1981), Cameron's (1975) or Loyn's (1977) position in favour of the massive migration of Scandinavians (including women and children) seems more satisfactory than that of Sawyer (1978), which proposes that there was

---

36   Smith (1935: 49-50).
37   "[896] Then the following summer, in this year, the host dispersed, some to East Anglia, some to Northumbria, and those without stock got themselves ships there, and sailed south oversea to the Seine". Tr. Garmonsway (1953: 89).

essentially a bunch of soldiers who dissolved into the native Anglo-Saxon population. The former posit that there is evidence for a secondary -or peasant- migration not very long after the armies conquered eastern England between 865 and 879, and the main idea of this hypothesis revolves around Lund's (1969: 196) claim:

> An examination of the armies, their behaviour, their size, their composition, as far as these problems can be elucidated, will show that the armies alone could not possibly have given rise to all these place-names or to linguistic influences of the kind in question. Hence we must conclude that the members of the armies were not the sole Danish immigrants who came to England during the years c. 865-c.925. A secondary migration must be presumed.

On the opposite side of the argument is Sawyer, maintaining that all the Scandinavian terms occurring in English –including place-names– were introduced by soldiers. According to this thesis, there is no evidence that other settlers from Scandinavia came, except some references to attacks from 980, and these are not connected with the "First Viking Age". However, the fact that most person-names included in compound place-names are Scandinavian may be seen as the antithesis of this (Cameron 1970: 38-ff). Were we to accept Sawyer's proposal, we would need to accept that this army, whose number of soldiers was estimated at around one thousand, was able to exert the kind of powerful influence on the Anglo-Saxon population and their language that Sawyer himself (1969: 171) describes, thus: "By then the language spoken in those parts of England was deeply affected by Scandinavian speech, and the names given to the new settlements reflected this Scandinavian influence".

Sawyer's position, which offering the similarity between the two languages as the only cause of change, seems insufficient. More recently, authors such as Dance (2003, 2011) have also referred to the similar linguistic constructions existing in both Old English and Old Norse, but they should not be the only factors to be taken into account since for language change to take place speakers are needed (Milroy 1997). Scarcity of evidence one way or the other might lead us to suppose that a second migration and a subsequent massive contact is a better explanation for what was to occur at a time in which there were no effective means of exerting influence on the linguistic habits of illiterate social groups. Cameron (1969:177) critiques Sawyer's premises in the following terms:

Mr. Sawyer will simply have to take our word for it that the Scandinavian languages affected the vocabulary of English dialects on a large scale, and that it also influenced the phonology, the syntax and the grammar too. If he wishes to argue that this was the result of the settlement of a small number of Danes in the East-Midlands for example, that is up to him, but he will have to provide something better than mere similarity of Old English and Old Danish to explain it.

Lund (1969: 197), in turn, proposes a comparison between the Norman and the Scandinavian influences on English:

> The best way of assessing the Danish linguistic influence in terms of settlement seems to be to compare it with the influence of the Normans. We know for certain that the Norman Conquest was an aristocratic one, it was an imposition of Norman owners upon English estates, it did not introduce a French peasant population into England. This conquest did not have very serious consequences for English place-names. Now, if the Danish influence on English place-names, the importance of which Mr. Sawyer himself admits, was effected in the way he thinks -through a later internal colonisation by English peasants whose language had been influenced by those few Danes from the armies who had settled in the neighbourhood as lords of the villages- why should we not expect an equally important French influence through the French aristocracy which superseded the Danish one?

And in reference to place-names he adds that the linguistic evidence as a whole seems to "justify the conclusion that the influx of Danish peasants into England, big enough to warrant the name of a migration, took place in the decades after 875" (Lund 1969: 197).

We should also bear in mind that the design of some Viking Age ships, as is the case of those known as *knorr*, took into account the need to transport not only sailors and warriors but also passengers and cattle. It is perfectly believable that such boats headed for Britain exactly as they headed for Iceland, Greenland, the North Atlantic Islands or any other territories colonised by the Scandinavians (Atkinson 1990: 22-24). Women used to travel in those boats on colonising trips, as we are told in the *Grænlendinga Saga* when Karlsefni tried to get to Vinland:

Hin sama var umræða á Vínlandsför sem fyrr og fýstu menn Karlsefni mjög þeirrar ferðar, bæði Guðríður og aðrir menn. Nú var ráðin ferð hans og réð hann sér skipverja, sex tigi karla og konur fimm.[38]

Chronicles also provide information about events that, generally speaking, coincide with the Second Migration and the military campaigns accompanying it. After the clashes between the natives and the Scandinavians, King Edward of Wessex managed to have all of Northumbria in English hands and the conditions under which his subjects lived at the time led to him being named "The Peaceful". However, peace was short-lived because under the reign of his heir, Æðelred Unræd, new Viking fleets arrived, this time in the South. In 991 a fleet of ninety-three ships led by Olaf Trygvasson came directly from Denmark. They won the well-known Battle of Maldon before heading to North across the Danelaw. There they were joined by some second and third generation Scandinavians, descendants of the men that had fought with Guthrum in the *micel here*. This treason on the part of the Northumbrians so angered King Æðelred that he had all foreigners outside the Danelaw killed. In this massacre (year 1002) Gunnhildr, sister of Sveinn Forkbeard, King of Denmark, was also killed. After learning of his sister's death, Sveinn gathered a fleet in 1007 and went to East Anglia, together with some Norwegians, to seek revenge. The battle was violent and continued until Æðelred fled to France. After Sveinn's death in 1014, the English king returned with the intention of containing the Danophiles, who claimed the English throne for Knutr, Sveinn's son.

As might be expected, Knutr took his ships to England to claim the throne, entering at the mouth of river From. From there, he crossed Wessex and Mercia towards York, the capital. Within a few months all of England, with the exception of London, was under Danish rule. When Æðelred died in 1016, Edmund Ironside resisted Knutr from London and they agreed to divide the territory in two once again, just as Alfred and Guthrum had done in the past. When Edmund died, Knut was crowned king of all England. Some of the men that had accompanied him now went back to Scandinavia but the rest remained and settled in England, this time also to the South and West of the

---

38 "He (Karlsefni) yielded and gathered sixty men and five women to go with him. They agreed to share equally in the profits and took livestock in order to make permanent settlement."

Danelaw.[39] Around 1028, Knutr reigned over the biggest empire in Northern Europe, including Denmark (which he had inherited from his brother Harald in 1019) and Norway. However, this *Danewæld* (North Sea Empire) was to be short-lived. Similar to what had happened to the Carolingian Empire after the Emperor's death, the *Danewæld* was divided between his sons, Harald and Hardeknut. Hardeknut inherited the throne of England, but when he died the English elected King Edward the Confessor, the half-Saxon half-French son of Æðelred Unræd.

During this period, now very close to what is generally considered the beginning of Middle English, further influxes of Scandinavians were seen in England. They came to protect their fellow countrymen from the French, which they considered a threat to their condition as "freemen". Notwithstanding their efforts, they finally had to abandon the population of Scandinavian descent in England to the Normans. From this moment onwards, a new cultural and linguistic ingredient began to exert its influence on the people and their language. However, the effects of the Normans are beyond the scope of this work.

5. Types of Scandinavian settlements in England

One of the main linguistic effects of the Scandinavian colonisation of England can be observed in place-names. From his detailed study of the toponymy of the Danelaw, Cameron (1953, 1959, 1965, 1969, 1970, 1971, 1975, 1977, 1978, 1985, 1990) established a taxonomy for the type of Scandinavian settlements that might have existed in the Danelaw. Of course we must be careful when using this evidence since there is no way we can know whether such place-names originated among the native population or were created by the newcomers.

> In using this evidence [place-names], we must remember that names given to inhabited sites were probably, on the whole, given by those who lived in the neighbourhood, rather than by those who lived in the places themselves... Of course, it does not follow that all names were given in this way, and Land-

---

39 It is worth noting that this process is parallel to the one that, according to the Chronicles we revised in the previous section, occurred during the First Migration when the memebers of the *micel here* became farmers.

námabók, the book of the settlement of Iceland, tells us that the settlers there did give names to their new homes (Cameron 1965: 4).

Although place-names do not always reflect the reality of the area where they are found, they may help us to have an idea of the type of community behind them and, thereby, the possible relationships and social networks established within them. Cameron provided figures from *Domesday Book* corresponding to the area under study (Finn 1968). It contains 109 Scandinavian place-names, 73% of which have a Danish name preceding the suffix. In this way he established that those place-names with the suffix *-thorp* usually correspond to places that, either due to their size or importance, were secondary to a place containing the suffix *-by*. The latter were generally identified as relatively important towns. In positing this theory, Cameron (1970: 37) argues that such place-names usually carry a direction indicator marker (he also takes into account the elements preceding the suffix in these compounds) such as "east", "south", etc. Whereas an important town might have an Anglo-Saxon name, whenever there are place-names with *-thorp* close by, I agree with Cameron (1970: 48) when he affirms:

> Now this seems to me to support the general hypothesis I have proposed that Danish settlement in the north-east Midlands was on a considerable scale, and was not simply the result of the settlement of a part of an army, itself to be counted only in hundreds.

The innovative aspect of this proposal, compared to other similar research, lies in his claiming that the suffixes used in place-names provide information regarding not only the size or importance of settlements, but also the date of creation in relation to other existing ones. With his classification of names ending in *-by*, *-thorp* and what he terms "Grimston-hybrids"[40], Cameron concludes that places with a "Grimston-hybrid" name are early settlements (con-

---

40 "Grimston-hybrid is a term which has been given to those place-names in which the first element is a Scandinavian personal name and the second element is OE *tun* 'a farmstead, a village'" (Cameron 1971: 147). Grimston-hybrids are formed with a Scandinavian name that is not usually found as such in the *Domesday Book* (and hence it is thought to have a very early origin and it is already outdated by the time the *Domesday Book* is written, in the eleventh century). Some of these names, later anglicised, are distributed exactly in the limits of areas with a high concentration of place-names with *-by*, but with numerous villages with an English name. Cf. Cameron, K. 1971.

trary to the general idea that they were late ones). They are areas where the Anglo-Saxons were already living before the Scandinavians arrived: in Cameron's words (1971: 160): "We must, in general, agree with Stenton that these hybrids represent earlier English villages, partially renamed by the Danes". Places whose names have a suffix such as *-by*, however, are new settlements resulting from a conscious colonisation rather than from the random choice of some hundreds of soldiers.

There is a coincidence in terms of topographical features: towns with an entirely Anglo-Saxon name as well as hybrid ones have a very similar topography, which may indicate one consistent criterion for selection on the part of their first settlers. Besides this, there is a very peculiar distribution of place-names. In his work on the Grimston-hybrids in Derbyshire, Cameron observes that hybrids outnumber names with *-by* or *-thorp* "where Danish settlement, in terms of names in *by*, is thickest, Grimston-hybrids are rare". (1971: 154). This seems to indicate that the Scandinavians did not need to find new settlements and give them new names (settlements with names with *-by*) in those places where already existing towns or villages took them in. Finally, place-names with the suffix *-thorp* seem to be smaller than those with *-by* and also seem to have been created later "pointing to a time when a greater integration had taken place between Dane and English. For instance, there are fewer Danish compound names and more hybrid names, part English, part Danish" (Cameron 1970: 41).

The idea defended by Cameron throughout his work is that the Scandinavian presence in England was not restricted to a limited number of military skirmishes, but that there existed a real movement of population from Northern Europe to the British Isles with the intention to settle and start a new life. This idea is quite reasonable if we take into account two main factors: on the one hand, the pressure by the Carolingian Empire on Northen Europe; on the other, the fact that there had been a coup de force in Denmark, making it impossible for those supporting King Harald Klak to return to Denmark. Available data, then, can be interpreted in the light of this theory and it can be considered that whereas a Scandinavian name does not always imply Scandinavian presence, the opposite may be also true (Cameron 1970: 48): "Now, if a *thorp* is indeed an outlier of a place with an English name, one could presumably deduce that the place of primary settlement had none the less received a number of Danish settlers, without the name being phonetically affected."

The more than two thousand Scandinavian place-names identified in England seem to reveal a more important settlement than previously considered and, as regards the number of settlers, they must have been many more than a group of fleeing soldiers, given that the *micel here* did not exceed one thousand men, many of whom may have returned to their homeland.

Likewise, according to the study of the distribution of these place-names, it could be affirmed that some kind of demographic pressure was exerted inland from the eastern coasts of England by the newcomers. According to Geipel (1971: 43), the impression of large influxes of newcomers arriving from Denmark after the conflicts between Alfred and Guthrum had ceased, yet these "colonists" may have exerted greater linguistic pressures and influences than what is traditionally believed to have been the case.

Chapter Two

The social structure

1. Social organisation in pre-Norse times

The social stratification for later periods of the history of England has been successfully reconstructed, and can provide sociolinguistic information useful to us. Such is the case with Nevalainen and Raumolin-Brunberg's (2003) work on Tudor and Stuart English, for which several sources were used. However, most of the information about how society was structured in England before the arrival of the Normans in 1066 is obtained from *Domesday Book*. Once he conquered England, William the Conqueror commissioned a group of officers to compile information about what kind of prerogatives and obligations his subjects had. This constituted a kind of census in which people, animals and things were recorded, and in this way the underlying social structure of the country is very well reflected indeed. *Domesday Book* also contains revealing information on both personal and place-names. Both personal and place-names, as well as those relating to geographical features, help us assess the extent to which the Scandinavian influence is felt in each place. It is important, however, to bear in mind that a Scandinavian personal name does not necessarily imply that its bearer is Danish or of Danish descent at all. Such names could simply have been fashionable among Anglo-Saxons. We know that Scandinavian things (clothes and hair-style) were considered highly fashionable among the Anglo-Saxon natives for a long time (Arbman and Binns 1961), and we must therefore agree with Cameron (1971: 149) when he affirms: "Their [these names] occurrence, therefore, is no indication of the racial origin of the men and women who bore them". Thus, whereas the many clearly Scandinavian names referring to people with certain privileges contained in *Domesday Book* for Derbyshire may mean that many of the socially relevant positions were held by Danes (and it is, after all, a Danelaw area), this might very well not be the case.

Domesday Book was compiled using a division of the Norman king's territory into different geographical areas that basically coincide with present-day counties. As a result of this it is easy to compare the organisation of different places in England, the Danelaw and elsewhere. According to a volume in Ely's Abbey, commissioners had to ask several questions in order to collect the information and prepare this sort of census. The questions were essentially the following (Morris 1978):

- The name of the place. Who held it, before 1066, and now?
- How many hides? How many ploughs, both those in the lordship's possession and those of men?
- How many villagers, cottagers, and slaves; how many free men and Freemen?
- How much woodland, meadow and pasture? How many mills and fishponds?
- How much has been added or taken away? What was and is the total value?
- How much each free man or Freeman had or has? All twofold, before 1066, when king William gave it and now; and if more can be had than at present?

Other documents, such as codes enacted by the king, grants and several types of legal texts, also offer a portrait of what Medieval England must have been like. In general, it is described as a feudal structure, but perhaps we should go back in time and also consider social situations not only prior to the Norman Conquest, but to the Scandinavian colonisation as well. In this way we will be able to understand more fully the changes that occurred with the coming of the so-called Vikings.

1.1. The monarchy

In the centuries preceding the coming of the Scandinavians the territories we now call England and Scotland were shared by several Celtic peoples. After a period of successive annexations and conquests by other tribes from the continent they were reduced to seven main kingdoms we know as the "Anglo-Saxon Heptarchy". The term Heptarchy is probably not very accurate since recent research has shown that some of the kingdoms never achieved the same status as others. Such was the case of Essex and Sussex. At the same time, alongside the seven kingdoms included in this Heptarchy, there were other political entities such as Bernicia and Deira within Northumbria and the Hwicce in the southwest Midlands, which seem to have had an important role, although in terms of the traditional historical perspective they have never been taken much into consideration.

The different kingdoms and federations (Jones 1998; Couper-Kuhlen, and Kortmann, 2000) had originated from the fifth century onwards as the result of the settlements of peoples with different geographical and ethnic provenance, all of them belonging to a common Germanic trunk:

> The first impression of early seventh-century England is that it was divided into large kingdoms: Kent, Sussex (the South Saxons), Wessex (the West Saxons), East Anglia, Essex (the East Saxons), Mercia (including the Middle Angles), and Northumbria (comprising Bernicia and Deira and, a little later, Lindsey). Reality was not quite so neat. Kingdoms were only gradually emerging from a state of flux: Middlesex, for instance, is probably the remains of a much larger Mid-Saxon territory dismembered before any surviving records could note it (Morgan 1989: 69).

Not all these ethnic groups are mentioned by Bede in his account. Besides Jutes, Angles and Saxons, other ethnic groups are mentioned by Orosius and other sources. They appear as *Bretwaldas* o *Brytenwaldas* (over-kings) in different territories that successively render their authority and power to the Anglo-Saxon peoples[41]. The Germanic tribes that little by little populated the Isles did not in fact have the extremely democratic organisation once attributed to them, this earlier misunderstanding due to a misinterpretation of certain elements relating to the *witan* or royal council. This error, made for example by Kemble and Liebermann in the nineteenth century, was to interpret the *witan* as a National Assembly. Some chronicles also contained misleading fragments such as OE *ceosan to cyninge* which in fact does not imply the existence of an election principle in the *witan* (Chadwick 1907). The royal council was in reality an aristocratic body whose members were nominated

---

41 The first settlers mentioned by Bede date back to 620 and even though we do not know what kind of authority they held, we do know they fought neighbour kingdoms (Morgan 1989: 71). We also know that men called *Bretwalda*, "...felt themselves entitled and able to interfere directly in the affairs of states which lay beyond the boundaries of their own kingdoms" (Blair 1970: 203). To a certain extent, the terms *cyning* and *ealdorman* designate a similar type of authority. It is in this general sense that I use the term "over-king".

by the king himself. Notwithstanding its most obvious etymological origin[42], *witenagemot* was the meeting of the royal councillors and not of the wise men.

On many occasions during the seventh century the king's council was formed by members of his house, in a broad medieval sense. Over the course of time the institution became more complex. However, the fact that a number of people accompanied the king did not imply they had a right to be consulted. According to authors such as Chadwick (1907) and/or Blair (1970: 217), this reflects the monarch's wish to make sure laws were observed more rigorously because they were made known and approved of by those who were more relevant to the kingdom. For this reason the Church was also deeply involved. In fact, OE *seonoð* (from Latin *synodus*) and *gemot* often appear as synonyms. Although *seonoð* does not necessarily refer to an ecclesiastical assembly, it may be indicative of the influence of the Church on the development of the royal counsel. In Blair's (1970: 221-222) words:

> It is not possible to define the membership of the council with any precision nor can its functions be exactly described. In practice it was concerned with the drawing up of laws, with the transfer of estates, with foreign affairs and the raising of taxes, and there were brief occasions when virtually the whole government of the country must have rested in its hands. It can hardly be doubted that a body of this kind played an important part in the work of government, particularly in the tenth and eleventh centuries, even though it never established its position so firmly by right that effective government could not continue without it.

1.2. The local governments

All the structure of local government in medieval England is based upon Anglo-Saxon and Scandinavian models. There is nothing left from Roman times. On the other hand, the Normans must be only granted a better and more efficient use of the already existing structures.[43] Even before the constitution of

---

42 *Witena* is the genitive plural of a weak noun whose first meaning is "one who knows" (Blair 1970: 216).

43 It would be realistic to think that both Anglo-Saxon and Scandinavian social schemes originated not in an interest for politics but in the need to be well organised for the paying of the tributes that primitive kings demanded, so that the burden was lighter for all subjects. The same type of organization was used to find men to fight for their king.

the Danelaw with the Treaty of Wedmore (878), the OE term *scir* is recorded to refer to a unit of local administration. As early as the first half of the ninth century, some personal names coinciding with those of present-day counties can be recognised. Although it is not easy to identify clear borderlines between these primitive counties one can suppose that many of them were sometimes fuzzy and were more clearly drawn in Alfred's times.

The origin of counties is diverse and can be attributed to the following causes:

1) For the East Midlands counties we can venture an entirely Danish origin and they would represent the division of those parts of Mercia conquered by the different units of the Danish army settling there. It is the confederation known as "Land of the Five Boroughs" including Derby, Nottingham, Leicester, Lincoln and Stamford.
2) Yorkshire constitutes a special case, since it more or less coincides with the area colonised by Halfdan from 876 (Second Migration), later on becoming a clearly different political entity from York's kingdom (ruled by Scandinavian kings).
3) Those counties we could label "West Saxon" seem to have originated from those areas first inhabited by the English invaders. Their aspect generally coincides with present-day limits.
4) Counties of an ecclesiastic origin, like Durham.
5) Cumberland and Northumberland represent two ancient Anglo-Saxon kingdoms.
6) Other Northern counties such as Lancashire and Westmorland appear more recently, around the thirteenth century.

The county can be considered the most important unit of government during the late Anglo-Saxon period since it was through the officers presiding over a county that the king could exert a considerable degree of control over local affairs. The county court's function was twofold: to communicate what the king commanded, and to solve any issues that were of great importance from a local perspective but of little or no interest to the centre of power[44]. *Eal-*

---

44 According to Blair (1970: 228) these local courts were functioning in Wessex in Alfred's times, but the first specific reference to a *scirgemot* appears in a grant by Edgar indicating it must meet twice a year under the bishop's and the *ealdorman*'s supervision to ensure the compliance of both secular and ecclesiastical law.

dormen were the royal officers placed in charge of counties, and were of aristocratic descent, sometimes belonging to the king's family. Although their posts were not a hereditary ones at the beginning, this changed little by little. Undoubtedly, one of the reasons for this change was the possibility for these officers to obtain great privileges (and lands) in exchange for their services. Among any *ealdorman*'s duties were the following: to lead the county's troops in times of war, to preside over the local court and to solve any problems there which were clearly local in nature, and to make sure that the king's orders transmitted as decrees were duly enforced (Loyn 1953: 513-525).

The number of *ealdormen* diminishes throughout the tenth century as their area of influence increases, even spreading across the frontiers of a single county. At the same time, the title *ealdorman* begins to transform into *eorl*, with the result that in the eleventh century an *ealdorman* or *eorl* is no longer the king's representative for legal affairs but has become a magnate whose possessions may include several counties and who may be as powerful as the king himself (Blair 1970: 228). This phenomenon is the result of accumulating privileges that consisted mostly of land possessions or exemption from taxes (leading to an accrual of wealth).

In order to occupy the administrative slot left by the *ealdorman*, another socially relevant figure appears. This is one of the king's *reeves*, the *scirgerefa* ("shire-reeve" or sheriff). This officer was recognised during Æðelred Unræd's reign as the county court president although the title is not recorded until Knut's times. Once again, this court's task is related to all aspects of local administration, both secular and religious, most of the issues dealt with having to do with land ownership.

South from Tees, counties were further sub-divided into smaller units, as recorded from the eleventh century onwards, called "hundreds" or "wapentakes". Both units served the same purpose and the fact that one or the other survived depended on whether it was Old English or Old Norse that had a greater influence on the area[45]. Again, "hundreds" predominate over "wapentakes", which were limited to the territory of the Five Boroughs, to York-

---

45   The term *wapentake* derives from OE *wæpentæc* which, in turn, comes from ON *vápnatak*. The latter belongs to legal terminology and was used in Scandinavian territories to refer "...to the act of seizing and brandishing weapons by those assembled at a meeting as a way of showing approval of a measure" (Blair 1970: 232). However, this is only used in an administrative sense in England.

shire's West Ridings, that is, a clearly Danish area. The "hundred" appears as a clear administrative unit with its own assembly from the tenth century onwards. According to extant documents, it would meet once every four weeks to pass sentence on thieves and to gather lost cattle. In Whitrelock's (1987: 138) words: "The meetings took place in the open, often at some prominent landmark that gave its name to the hundred; barrows served this purpose at Babergh, Suffolk, Ploughley and Cheneward'berge, Oxfordshire; trees or stones at Appletree, Derbyshire, Staine, Cambridgeshire, etc."

Hundreds had a principal officer (OE *hundredesmann*) who had to be informed in cases of theft so that he could, in turn, inform the men in the *tithings*[46] who had to apprehend the thief. Anybody who did not meet their duties towards the hundred had to pay a fine to the hundred itself and to the lord. Fines could be also imposed for not attending the hundred's court. If any matter, involving either men or cattle, transcended the hundred's frontiers it was necessary to inform the neighbouring *hundredesmann* so that he could organise and carry out the required actions.

As regards the "wapentake", although there are no grants or laws referring exclusively to it, there is a code enacted by Æðelred Unræd in Wantage. This document makes reference above all to the Five Boroughs and admits the existence of a court hierarchy: first, the Five Boroughs court itself, presided by the *ealdorman* (or the corresponding king's officer); second, each of the boroughs' courts, independent from each other; finally, the "wapentake" court. Each "wapentake" must be formed by twelve *thegna* who are in charge of arresting anyone prosecuted by the king's officer. In Whitelock's (1987: 138) words:

> Ethelred the Unready issued at Wantage a code intended to supress lawlessness and violence in the North. It imposes very heavy fines for a breech of the king's peace, and it employs a method of bringing malefactors to justice that is probably derived from Scandinavian law: <<An assembly is to be held in each wapentake, and the twelve leading thanes and with them the reeve are to go out and swear on the relics which are placed in their hands that they will accuse no guiltless man nor conceal any guilty one. And they are to arrest the men frequently accused, who are at issue with the reeve.>>.

---

46   It is not clear whether the *Tithing* refers to police-like groups of men in this context or if, rather, it involves some kind of territorial subdivision of the "hundred". Both OE *þing* and ON *þing* mean "meeting".

There is abundant information about this Scandinavian, not Anglo-Saxon, origin of this aristocratic body. The group of twelve "doomsmen" is often mentioned both in Scandinavian literature and history and its antiquity is enhanced by the belief (also expressed in Scandinavian mythology) that there were also twelve gods. It is not easy to know the exact mission of these dozen men but it seems to be similar to that of a jury.[47] Two or three of them, always after taking an oath, were present in trade transactions both as witnesses and to avoid the sale of stolen goods or cattle. Generally speaking, the thanes had to be informed about any action related to trade on the part of the hundred's inhabitants.

We can affirm that the functions of the English-descended twelve men in the hundred were not exactly the same as those of their equivalent in the "wapentake" with its clear Scandinavian influence. Therefore, the difference in the terms used is mirrored by a socio-historical difference, as can be inferred from Æðelred's and Edgar's law codes, respectively. The hundred's men were mere witnesses in commercial exchanges whereas those in the "wapentake" constituted a jury with the twofold mission of arresting and judging people. In this sense, the latter can be compared to another group of twelve men denominated *judices* or *lagemanni*. Some traces of these *lagemanni* appear in Cambridge, Stamford, Lincoln, York and Chester, all of them places under Scandinavian influence. There is great variation in the size of hundreds in different geographical areas and their frontiers were less stable than those of the county. However, it is important to distinguish between the hundred as a measure of land and as a fiscal unit. As a unit of measure, a hundred is equivalent to 100 "hides"[48], but from a tax perspective a hundred is the extension of land producing the equivalent as one hundred hides even if it is not that large.

We must finally consider a territorial unit which can be placed between the county and the "hundred" or the "wapentake". It is the *thridings* (from ON *þriðjungr*), whose present-day heirs are the Ridings in Yorkshire and Lindsey. It seems that the term ON *þriðjungr* stands for "the third part", so

---

47 A passage in *Wantage code* affirms that a veredict (OE *dom*) in which all thanes agree will be considered valid, but if it is not unanimous the opinion of eight if them will be regarded as valid and the other four will be paid a fine (Blair 1970).
48 For a detailed account of the "hide" see 2.1. below.

that we might infer that it will often make reference to the third part of the bigger unit (the "hundred" or the "wapentake"). As explained by Blair (1970: 240), each of these units had its own assembly: "The system of a unit and its subdivisions, represented only by the riding in England, is found almost universally in countries occupied by Scandinavian peoples during the Viking Age. The riding or third part is found in Orkney, as well as in parts of Norway and Sweden."

2. Social organisation of the field in non-Scandinavian areas

Different terms referring to what we would call a farm or small village nowadays were in use during the Middle Ages in England. One of them was OE *tun* (Latin *villa*) which was used for any plot of land that was conveniently delimited and fenced. The term could also designate the group of people living within it. In the eastern counties the term *ham*, denoting a smaller extension of land than a *tun* was used. OE *wic*, from Latin *vicus*, developed the meaning of PE *village*, but it kept the meaning of "farm" in some compounds. The words *worðig* and *worðign*, still to be found in many place-names, referred to smaller places. Together with these nouns there are traces of Scandinavian influence in place-names, as we will see in chapter two, almost all of them referring to this type of farm, as is the case with OE *by* (ON *byr*, *bær*; Swedish and Dan. *by*), *þorp*, etc.

Although our knowledge of Anglo-Saxon society is extremely limited due to a lack of documentation, we do know it was constituted upon two basic and complementary elements contained in the phrase *ge eorle ge ceorle*: the *ceorl* and the lord[49]. No reason why the lord is the lord and the *ceorl* is the *ceorl* has been found. Notwithstanding this, we do have information about their functions, which varies in the different geographical areas.

The whole agricultural system, that is, all the economy, is organised around the possessions and influence of a lord, be this religious (a community or a bishop) or not. Such estates (referred to with the French terms *manor* or *demesne* in *Domesday Book*) were inhabited by men and women whose work was supervised by an officer appointed by the lord, identified as *gerefa* (PE

---

[49] The original OE term has been kept here since it could not be satisfactorily rendered into any other present-day English word.

reeve, bailiff) in extant documents. The officer's work was very complex since he had to know all the rights and duties of both lord and workers. He also had to be informed about the best moment of the year to perform each task (sowing, reap, fishing, cattle-related tasks, etc.) in order to obtain the best results, and he was also in charge of the lord's household.

Among the men and women under the officer's supervision were both *ceorlas* and serfs. The extensive available information relating to the former allows us in what follows to offer a brief description of their varied roles throughout the British Isles; by contrast, serfs seem to have a more or less similar role across the whole territory.

2.1. The ceorle. Status and evolution in time

Although I have decided to keep the OE term, it has been translated in various ways in the literature as PE *husbandman, freeman, commoner, peasant* and *villein*[50]. In all cases it refers to a free man since, contrary to what happens with serfs, he had certain legal rights, including to inherit, to bequeath, and to rent or sell properties. They also had the duty of paying taxes to the Church. Unlike serfs, they were not bond to the land so that they were not included as a part of land transactions. Most *ceorlas* were farmers (not only peasants, but also shepherds, beekeepers, etc.), but they could also be craftsmen or tradesmen. However, through the acquisition of lands or prosperity in their business they could climb the social ladder as far as the lowest ranks of the aristocracy. On occasions, the reverse occurred, with war, crop fail or any other adverse circumstance obliging these free men to ask a lord for help in exchange for part of their freedom (see below). The *wergild*, or fine to be paid by anyone killing a *ceorl*, was considerably higher than that of a serf, and thus he stood in an intermediate position between nobility and serfdom.[51]

---

50 In *Domesday Book* they are sometimes called *villani* and sometimes *bordarii*. The translation "villein" seems not to be the most accurate one since, from the Norman Conquest onwards, the term was also used to refer to a man who was not free.

51 For a detailed account of *wergild* and its relevance at the time, see Whitelock 1987.

According to different documents[52], the figure of the *ceorl* is so complex that we can find different ranks within it. They correspond, basically, to the following scheme:

GENEAT: It is possible that a *geneat* had to pay his lord a rent for the land he occupied as well as a specific amount for the use of common fields. He also participated in the payment of alms and had to perform certain additional jobs for the lord, jobs which could be very different from one estate to the other, but were always "inland". They could often be certain tasks regarded as "honourable". His property was usually equivalent to one hide[53].

GEBUR: He possessed a fourth of a hide or yarland[54] that he received from his lord together with furniture, implements and some domestic animals. When he died, all those things and animals returned to the possession of the lord. The *gebur* had to do certain agricultural jobs on the lord's lands besides paying him a rent.

COTSETLA: He occupied the lowest position among *ceorlas*. He owned five acres of land and, unlike *geneatas* and *gebuas*, did not pay a rent. He had to work on the lord's properties and also to work as a watchman. Although his status was very low, he was still free because he was subject to the payment of religious taxes.

These social nuances can be better seen in Graph 1, below. It represents the social organisation of a prototypical community in the Danelaw during

---

52 My classification is based on the one proposed by Blair (1970) using four documents from the manors of Hurstbourne Priors in Hampshire, Tiddenham in Gloucestershire, a treatise on the organisation of estates entitled *Rectitudines Singularum Personarum* and a treatise on the duties of a *gerefa* entitled *Be Gesceadwisarz Gerefan*.

53 A hide is the amount of land necessary to keep a family during one year. In Bede's *Historia Ecclesiastica* the term used is Latin *terra unius familiae,* it does not have a particular extension, but it varies depending on the soil's conditions and the average standard of living in the area. In Kent the *sulung* was used instead of the hide. In fact, a *ceorl* in Kent had a social position which was better than in other parts of the country, as revealed by his *wergild.*

54 The fourth part of the Kentish *sulung* is the *yoke* (OE *geoc*).

Knutr's reign (1016-1035) once the Scandinavians had become well established in England.

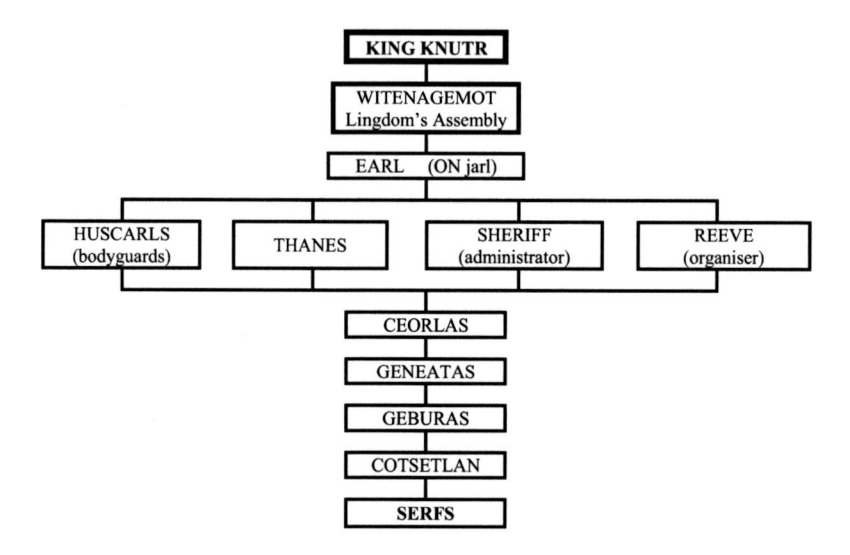

```
                    ┌─────────────┐
                    │ KING KNUTR  │
                    └──────┬──────┘
                    ┌──────┴──────────┐
                    │  WITENAGEMOT    │
                    │Lingdom's Assembly│
                    └──────┬──────────┘
                    ┌──────┴──────────┐
                    │ EARL  (ON jarl) │
                    └──────┬──────────┘
      ┌─────────────┬──────┴──────┬─────────────┐
┌─────┴──────┐ ┌────┴────┐ ┌──────┴──────┐ ┌────┴────┐
│ HUSCARLS   │ │ THANES  │ │   SHERIFF   │ │  REEVE  │
│(bodyguards)│ │         │ │(administrator)│ │(organiser)│
└────────────┘ └─────────┘ └──────┬──────┘ └─────────┘
                            ┌─────┴──────┐
                            │  CEORLAS   │
                            └─────┬──────┘
                            ┌─────┴──────┐
                            │ GENEATAS   │
                            └─────┬──────┘
                            ┌─────┴──────┐
                            │  GEBURAS   │
                            └─────┬──────┘
                            ┌─────┴──────┐
                            │ COTSETLAN  │
                            └─────┬──────┘
                            ┌─────┴──────┐
                            │   SERFS    │
                            └────────────┘
```

3. Society and the economy in the Danelaw. Scandinavian influence in the social fabric

Those relations established between the native population and colonisers[55] must be approached very carefully and information must be dealt with carefully too. This applies not so much to the information obtained from archaeological evidence as that from contemporary written records. The history of the Viking presence in England that has come down to us was written by their enemies and for this reason is not completely reliable[56]. Thus, Æthelweard, ealdorman of Wessex during the reign of Æðelred Unræd, wrote a chronicle of the past in which he refers to the Scandinavian in very harsh terms, in contrast to the sagas, in which the same events are reported from a heroic perspective. The heroic character of the Scandinavians is indeed never reflected

---

55 The use of this term instead of "invaders" is conscious and reflects my intention to follow Cameron's line of argument.
56 Blair's words (1970: 55) "...it should not be forgotten that the Vikings, whose very name is synonymous with pyracy, themselves introduced the word law into the English language" illustrate the tendency to regard any Scandinavian as a Viking.

in the English chronicles, yet it is found in archaeological remains, as Page (1987: 4) suggests when he affirms that "The memorial stones record a society that was in some ways self-consciously aristocratic, and a way of life that was in some ways self-consciously heroic". However, Æthelweard's chronicle, like the one by Asser in *Life of King Alfred*, is clearly derogative. According to Page (1987) the perspective adopted in the *Anglosaxon Chronicle* is more objective although the commercial intentions of many Scandinavians during the Viking Age is never mentioned there either, thus implying objective. The commercial tradition of the Scandinavians is nowadays well-known to have had two significant centres in Hedeby (Denmark) and Birka (Sweden). Large, prosperous communities existed in both cities that could be considered the antecedent of Hanseatic cities. The omission of these details in the written records tended to enhance the idea of the Viking pirate raiding civilised Europe from his own dark, primitive and heathen world.

More than a century later, Henry of Huntingdon tried to produce a work of a more historiographical nature, with less rhetorical effectiveness. According to Page (1987: 15) Henry sees the Danes as part of God's overall plan for putting Britain in its place and building a multi-racial society. William of Malmesbury, a contemporary of Henry of Huntingdon, seems to be more interested in describing England's social organisation and deals with the apparition of the Danes almost as a marginal phenomenon, though not underestimating their power; in fact, they are described as vicious, treacherous and cruel. However, William of Malmesbury acknowledges the Scandinavians have an important virtue in their loyalty to their lord[57]. There was also a chronicle in York which accounted for events from a completely different perspective from the other versions of the *Anglo-Saxon Chronicle* (Arbman 1961). It is clear that all these documents must be taken into consideration in an effort to reconstruct a highly complex reality.

There are many studies on the socio-economic and organisational differences between the Danelaw and the rest of the English territory. One of the pioneering works was by Stenton, who at the beginning of the twentieth century dealt with the description and analysis of these differences and whose claims seem to be as valid today as they were then. He affirms (1920: XIII)

---

[57] "In the early eleventh century there was at least one chronicler who recognised the Vikings as heroes even while describing their atrocities" (Page 1987: 26).

that in the shires of the Yorkshire border and the Welland, the ancient territory of the Five Boroughs, a social system which may be compared in essential terms to the Scandinavian settlement of the ninth century was least affected by the shock of the Norman Conquest or the obscurer process of subsequent internal change. Once the Scandinavians settled in East Anglia, some fortifications were built and occupied by small armies as permanent protection. According to Cameron, and as already pointed out above, it is with the protection of these armies that the Second Migration from Northern Europe took place. These citadels were placed in the so-called Territory of the Five Boroughs, the boroughs being present-day Derby, Leicester, Nottingham, Stamford and Lincoln. It seems that they were regarded as independent from one another:

> We do not know very much about the internal organisation or politics of the Vikings after this settlement, but there does not seem to have been very close contacts or indeed co-operation between the boroughs, still less of any central royal power. Each borough seems to have looked after its own affairs and to have had its own earl or king as leader. This is the impression conveyed also by the coinage which began to be issued in the Danelagu shortly before 890. (Lund 1969: 199)

Until the eleventh century both the society and economy in the Danelaw revolves, as is the case throughout the Middle Ages, around the ownership of land and its exploitation. Everyday life tied to the land takes place behind the protective shield of the small armies in the boroughs. In the Danelaw, land is measured in units called *bovates* (from Latin), more or less equivalent to twenty acres, a considerable amount of land, although not exactly the same everywhere. Individual properties vary from two bovates to one half, which means that peasant population did not possess great extensions of land but rather seem to have owned medium-size or small plots, although a *carucate size* (eight *bovates*, sixty-four hectares) is recorded in some documents. Thus, Stenton (1920: XX) states that "The local draftsman will generally avoid the word carucate even when he is describing a very considerable property". Instead of this term, the native *ploxland* (OE *plogesland*), a Scandinavian formation to denote the amount of land which could be tilled by one plough team, is usually preferred. A *plogesland* or *bovate* was divided into eight *oxgangs* (the oxen needed for a plough). This East Anglian system contrasts with the one in the rest of England, where the acre was the unit used.

As can be inferred from the information in *Domesday Book*, there used to be an open field to each side of a village. These were often divided in the same number of acres on both sides. There were also some plots of land that did not fall into the bovate system but which were divided (as can be inferred from charters) between these open fields. Therefore, the difference between a bovate with twenty acres or the same extension scattered in different plots is that which is reflected in documents under the labels of *demesne* (*inland*) for the former and *bovate* (*gesette land*) for the latter. Any plot had the right to use the common pastures, as well as a portion of meadow, a vegetable garden (*croft*) and a toft. According to Stenton (1920) numerous charters illustrate that the toft was the plot containing the house and buildings that belonged to the arable farm; it is exceptional for an arable tenement to be given without a toft as its appurtenance.

There seems to be a strict correspondence between the size of the arable tenement and the number of *tofts* recorded as an appendix and usually in the village itself, so that each owner can use the common rights in accordance with the amount of land he owns. This rule is seldom recorded in texts. Almost all these *tofts* are inhabited by cottagers (*cotsetla*). This social group constitutes an element complementing the distribution of arable land in big estates. There are several factors favouring its existence. One of them is the limit both to the number of men who can be employed to work in a single farm as well as to the profitable subdivision of tenements. This implies that a family's youngest son who does not wish to migrate must be provided with a plot where he may live by independent labour. Communities of free husbandmen produced such people in the same way as manors created groups of dependent cottagers for the cultivation of its demesne. This process seems to be the inevitable way in which individuals adjust to the economic system that made a difference between free farmers (sometimes called "villain") and those who finally became serfs to their lord ("cottagers").

The way in which land is distributed marks one of the main differences between the Danelaw and the rest of England. In fact, according to Stenton (1920: XLVIII) "The Danelagu in general, Lincolnshire in particular, was a region full of small landholders with the power of alienating their tenements in whole or in part, a power of which they were already taking advantage at an early date". Some scholars argue that the information extracted from contemporary sources seems to indicate that non-Scandinavian England had a higher number of cottagers and slaves (Kristenssen 1975). Others, however, hold the opposite opinion, that the only Scandinavians in England were those belonging to the *micel here*. This is the case of Sawyer (1969: 170) who affirms that the contrast between the Danelaw (with a substantial free peasantry) and the rest of the country "was not as sharp as *Domesday Book* makes it appear. In short, it should be recognised that the freemen and the *sokemen* of the Danelagu are no guide to the initial settlement of Scandinavians in Britain". Another distinctive feature between the two territories is the use of money. In contrast to the rest of the country, in the Danelaw money was used by people for ordinary purposes, and this could have been due to the fact that a considerable number of estates were held by free men at a money rent (Stenton 1920).

In the twelfth century some innovations were introduced in the socio-economic field. In the first place, new religious houses were founded to replace the ones that had disappeared either due to decadence, mentioned by Ælfred of Wessex in his Preface to the translation of the *Cura Pastoralis* (Sweet 1958: 2), or to the Viking raids. In England, as well as throughout Europe, rich people donated lands to these houses. The main difference is that in the Danelaw such donations were small plots, as can be deduced from the records of different monasteries. The fact that religious houses in the Danelaw never had great extensions of land but rather scattered plots, seems to confirm the theory that these were not donated by one single owner, as could be expected at a moment in which Norman rule was beginning to have its effects, but by many different small owners. It is not until the following century that the power over a village is concentrated in one single religious or lay under-tenant so that it becomes a feud or manor. Even in those cases, "the unity of the village was independent of the organisation of the manor" (Stenton 1920: LX).

Likewise, it is significant that scribes and clerks in the Danelaw systematically avoid using the word *manor* although *manerium, soke* and *berewick* appear in the sections of *Domesday Book* devoted to this region. It is obvious that the king's commissioners in charge of collecting the information are responsible for the use of these southern terms[58]. It is, indeed, impossible to ignore the varied evidence which reveals the village and not the manor as the essential form of rural organisation in this region (Stenton 1920: LXI). No authority of seigniorial origin controlled the whole economic life of these villages under divided lordship.

The concentration of land affects all sorts of properties whenever it occurs: there is no difference between a church, for instance, and other annexes generating rent. In fact, the seigniorial divisions of a village were often reproduced in the ecclesiastical sphere by a corresponding partition of the village church. In order to avoid its land going to another lord, religious houses obtained documents from each donor. However, in contrast with the idyllic idea of a democratic Germanic society formed by free men, in the Danelaw there are some signs of the existence of a system of serfdom, to be found in the use of terms such as *rustici, nativi, villani*. There are also some instances of transactions of men that do not refer to serfdom but to different relations of homage.

The social organisation of England in general, and that of the Danelaw in particular, can be represented in the following way. The information in *Domesday Book* tells us that there are certain men who have become lords because they accumulated lands before the arrival of the Normans. Afterwards, privileges are granted to those who accompanied William from the Continent. They received land in reward for their help during the Conquest[59]. Both the *reeve* (officer acting as witness in all kinds of transactions) and the *sokemen*, whose relation with the lord is paid for with money, not in services as is the

---

58   It is more reasonable to consider this as a problem of nomenclature than to think that manors existed in the eleventh century, at the time *Domesday Book* was written, disappearing later. It would not be surprising that King William's commissioners tended to use the terms they were familiar with to designate a type of reality similar to the one they knew in Normandy.

59   "Domesday Book is a record of a land deeply marked by the scars of conquest. In 1086 there were only two surviving English lords of any account. More than 4,000 thegns had lost their lands and been replaced by a group of less than 200 barons" (Morgan 1989: 121). This may be evidence of the extent to which lands were concentrated as I suggest elsewhere in this chapter.

case on the Continent and in other parts of England, are free men in their relation to their lord[60].

Great numbers of *sochemani liberi homines* (also *freemen*[61]) are mentioned in *Domesday Book*. Although they have many obligations, these men also have some rights regarding the land and their personal status. This could suggest they are some kind of aristocracy comparable to the *ceorles* in the rest of England. However, their social superiority is not accompanied by an economic superiority. The size of their plots may be different although they are always referred to as *soke*. There is another type of free man, the artisans, whose properties are located within the village. Both independent ploughmen and craftsmen possess a complement to their wealth consisting of a plot with a cottage, and cottagers to work it. As already mentioned, cottagers constitute a social group close to serfdom since they have no property and on occasions the only way they could pay their debts was by offering themselves as serfs (cf. *cotsetla* above). The lowest step on the social ladder is that of *rustici*, *nativi* and *villani* who are, in the end, slaves to other men.

The changes to be observed in texts from the eleventh to the thirteenth century may be due not only to a change in the social reality but to a shift in the lexicon and its meaning. Therefore, socio-historical conclusions must be carefully dealt with.

4. Towns and commercial activity

Sociolinguistic studies generally coincide as to the importance of the linguistic consequences of the type of population and grouping of speakers. Towns tend to be considered as particularly different elements for many studies nowadays, especially if the population under survey is irregularly distributed

---

60   The Normans may have kept this practice of accepting money instead of services.
61   The two main meanings for this term in *MED* come from OE *freomon, frigmon* and they are:
   a) a free man (as opposed to a bondman); one of the freeborn gentry (as opposed to a villain or serf) ; one who holds land in free tenure, a freeholder.
   b) a manumitted slave, a freedman.

among urban and non-urban contexts[62]. The former have always had characteristic socio-economic features, and, consequently, cultural ones too. This can also be applied broadly to medieval English towns. Cities as they had been during the Roman occupation had disappeared before the coming of the first Germanic tribes in the fifth century. In a basically agricultural context, with its corresponding linguistic effects, the idea of urban life does not correspond very much to our present-day concept.

There were three different OE terms to describe a community bigger than a *tun* or *ham*, usually organised around a trade centre. Such three terms are *burh* (a fortified place[63] where kings, bishops or important members of the nobility lived), *port* (towns with a right to have an official market and a mint) and *ceaster*, from Latin *castra* (urban-like centres already known in Roman times). From the tenth century onwards, the terms *burh* and *port* were often used for the same type of communities. Although there is no agreement as to the date in which towns and cities appeared, it seems they do not originate during the Roman period but later, some time before the arrival of the Scandinavians.

Such market-towns were important not only as a driving force for economic development, but also as places of linguistic intercourse. Some authors (Hines 1984) claim that a very tight commercial contact existed between England and Europe in the pre-Viking period. Archaeological findings testify to this and in Blair's (1970: 282) words "...at no time in its subsequent history has England been more closely united with the maritime countries of northwestern Europe than it was in the second half of the fifth and in the sixth centuries". Some market-towns could mint their own coins, and we have evidence that the Five Boroughs in the Danelaw certainly functioned as independent political units, since each of them had its own mint, just as the different kings of the so-called Anglo-Saxon Heptarchy had also had[64].

---

62   In this sense, the research carried out by Fernández-Rodríguez (1983, 1994, 1995) shows a difference between the seven Galician cities and non-urban areas since socio-economic peculiarities seem to have important linguistic consequences.
63   The defensive system built by King Alfred had these type of structures (citadels) labelled *burhs* in the *Burghal Hidage* his successor Edward the Elder commanded.
64   In relation to market-towns it is worth mentioning the importance of the twelve jury men or officers of the "hundred" or "wapentake". They acted as witnesses of commercial transactions at the market. King Edward the Elder promulgated a law in

Commercial exchange involves some kind of linguistic intercourse as a means of communicating transactions. It is also in this commercial context that we find divergent measure systems between areas densely populated with Scandinavians and the rest of the territory. Such differences have a particular lexical consequence. Besides *pund*, we soon find the English *scilling* and *penny*, the Scandinavian *mark* (OE *marc, mearc*; ON *mork*) and *ore* (OE *ora*; ON *eyrir*), which was an eighth of a *mark*. These differences complicated exchanges between Scandinavians and English, and one of the actions to reduce differences was the use of the *pondus hustingiae Londoniensis* and the *hustinges gewiht* ("pound of the London husting" and "husting weight", respectively, Blair 1970: 298). These suggest the existence of a court which was in charge, among other things, of regulating the markets and finding a unified nomenclature for them. There were other courts or assemblies to regulate trading activities, the frequency with which they met depending on the king. The two most important of these were in London and York.

The social structure we have now described, plus the different uses therein, explain a particular type of relationship among the inhabitants of medieval England which will determine social behaviour. Since language is a social phenomenon, the linguistic consequences of such behaviour can help explain certain aspects of the evolution of English that cannot be accounted for without considering language contact.

---

which no goods could be bought or sold outside these towns, that way increasing their social relevance as meeting places.

Chapter Three

The sociolinguistic perspective and related studies

1. Introduction

Once the socio-historical basics have been presented it is necessary to look at the main sociolinguistic models available before applying the one or more of them to the analysis of the linguistic situation of mediaeval Britain. Although very briefly, we must also consider certain concepts that are inevitably involved in a study of this kind, such as language change, lexical borrowing (some reference to lexico-semantic studies cannot be avoided) as well as pidgins and creoles. A reference to historical sociolinguistics in general and to the contribution of some authors in particular will be also found in what follows.

I will also try to define several key concepts here, although they have all been repeatedly mentioned in the literature, including *speech community*, *bilingualism* and *diglossia*. All will be dealt with here in order to provide a clear portrait of a situation that has been unique in the development of the English language.

2. Three fundamental models

No robust model for contact-induced language change has been provided yet (Siemund 2008) but some sociolinguistic approaches presented in the second half of the twentieth century seem to offer a valid starting point for its study. I will focus here on the study of those variation models proposed by Labov and Bailey, and the social network model of Milroy, since all three have been widely used and discussed. Ideas concerning the relationships between languages and societies that can be inferred from other theoretical frameworks, such as those of Saussure or Chomsky, will not be dealt with, since they consider both language and human beings at an individual level rather than from a collective, social perspective.

2.1. Labov's model

Sociolinguistics gains its empirical foundations from the sixties onwards, the moment at which William Labov breaks with the orthodox idea that language change occurs as an internal process of linguistic systems, instead formulating the theory that there exists interaction between speech and social structures. Many of the concepts and methods that were to infuence subsequent sociolinguistic studies were formulated in his 1966 work *The Social Stratification of English in New York City*. Labov's approach maintains that language is a heterogeneous entity formed by a set of socially structured variables. Such structured variables are analysed by Labov, who employs the quantitative methods of another discipline, Sociology. Indeed, *sociolinguistic variable* is one of the key concepts used by this author. It is understood as the group of different ways of expressing the same content, the set of alternatives having a different social meaning, each of these different alternatives being a *variant*.

The interaction between speech and social structure is essentially due to the fact that speech functions either as a differentiating element in social behaviours (speech constitutes a social variable in itself) or it functions as a control, pressure or prestige norm mechanism. This interaction accounts in many cases for those elements in language change that cannot be accounted for by resorting to the laws formulated by traditional historical linguistics, as is the case with Grimm's and Verner's Laws for the explanation of consonant mutations in Germanic languages. Labovians consider that the study of present-day phonological changes are valid tools for the study of those that occurred in the past, since they claim that the forces motivating change are similar at any given historical period. That is to say, the causes originating change are usually constant throughout the history of a language. Similarly, the social distribution of the different values of a particular variable (sex, age, social class, income, education, etc.) allow for the observation of language change as it is occurring and the direction it is taking. Nevertheless, it is evident that variables do not have an entirely permanent character, since what is regarded as fundamental for a present-day urban society (as in the case of twentieth-century New York) may not have been so in a medieval rural society (as in the case of an eleventh-century village nearby Nottingham).

The analysis of the different variants gives place to the concepts of "class stratification" and "style stratification". In fact, variation is not limited to society: all speakers vary their idiolect depending on the communicative situation in which they are immersed at different moments. This is what Labov labels "style variation" and it reflects the interaction between sender and receiver from the sender's point of view, taking into consideration that this type of variation modifies the way in which data is retrieved. In our case, since the data is from written sources, the values for style variation are not really important since, on the one hand, style is hardly altered except for the type of text we are dealing with in each instance and, on the other, there is no way we can have evidence of any interaction between sender and receiver.

When Labov studied language change in Martha's Vineyard, he observed the linguistic behaviour in two generations of speakers and this brought him to the consideration that it is possible to measure the language change occurring in the past from the observation of the present. Thus, he argues that there are, besides the postulates of traditional grammar, a series of factors that foster change and that these are not linguistic elements defined by their cognitive function. He accounts for this as follows (1972: 181):

> Internal, structural pressures and sociolinguistic pressures act in systematic alternation in the mechanism of linguistic change. It can no longer be seriously argued that the linguist must limit his explanation of change to the mutual influences of linguistic elements defined by cognitive function. Nor can it be argued that a changing linguistic system is autonomous in any serious sense.

Labov and his followers consider that language change always occurs in three phases:

1.–At the beginning, change appears only as the existence of one of the multiple variants of a form whose use is restricted to a particular social group. This is known as an indicator. The speakers promoting this change are not conscious of that fact and therefore no style stratification (the premeditated use of that particular variant in particular situations) is recorded.

In the history of English, two alternative pronunciations of the cluster <g> + front vowel may have been variants, although "standard" Old English contained only one. The new plosive one (of Scandinavian origin) is an indicator.

2.–This variant form then spreads and competes with the form which until then had been used by most speakers. When it is adopted by the speech community, this variant is called a marker[65]. It now begins to show style stratification, although it is still something speakers do unconsciously.

To return to our previous example, we can suppose the change in the pronunciation of <g> + front vowel as a plosive is a spread. In this way, two pronunciations co-exist in such examples as OE *giefan* as /ji(e)van/ and as /gi(e)van/, the latter now being a marker.

3.–Finally, the change reaches its culminatation. The form becomes regular and the competing variants are eliminated.

In our example, the change is completed when the palatal pronunciation disappears (Blockley 2008: 19). In fact, it is the velar one that survives in PE.

The important thing is that the new form, as well as the old ones, are now charged with social significance. In general terms, language change is the result of the social pressure exerted by a particular group, in a descending or ascending direction. Most likely it will begin in the middle ranks of society, since they are linguistically more unstable and less confident (Labov 1972). When Labov talks about change from above or from below he is not, in principle, referring to the social orientation of such a change, but to whether it is taking place from above or below the level of awareness of speakers. He affirms that almost all changes are changes from below (unconscious), but if the change is not started by a social group belonging to the higher ranks and if the variant predominating when the change is completed is not accepted by that group, then that form becomes stigmatised and due to a process of (conscious) hyper-correction a change from above begins. In cases in which stigmatisation of a form is noteworthy, it becomes a topic for conversation in what is labelled as a stereotype. Stereotypes are popularly-known and characteristic linguistic features "which tend not to show regular stratification, because everyone is so aware of them that they are often avoided by the very group of people they were once characteristic of" (Patrick 2011). Such a form

---

65   As suggested by Fasold (1990: 266), the difference between indicators and markers depends on the definition Labov offers for speech community as a group sharing values concerning language regulations. Such definition allows him to differentiate between a speech community and its sub-groups.

may subsequently disappear or remain as a variable with no further changes. Given the character of the present work it is virtually impossible to provide this type of information. We can only know that a particular form has been stigmatised when the author of a particular text refers to it in some sort of jocular way, and even here the form in question may be stigmatised for a particular author whereas not for others.

If change is originated in the upper social groups (which seldom occurs), the new variant is not usually stigmatised. On the contrary, it becomes a prestige form. Likewise, if the variant originates in the lower groups, it may be accepted by the upper groups and not stigmatised, in which case it may also acquire prestige and be used in formal settings. In the case of Anglo-Scandinavian it is probable that change occurred at both ends: from power in the cities of the Five Boroughs and from the most humble classes in the country.

According to what has been said up to this point, although not all cases of variability imply linguistic change, it is true that linguistic change needs variability. In fact, those most deeply involved in the history of the language than in other aspects of it, as is the case of M. L. Samuels, tend to show interest in these sociolinguistic theories. Samuels (1989: 113) affirms that "spoken Scandinavian survived, in closed communities, till the twelfth century in the focal area". As these communities opened up[66] language change appeared: the generation of younger speakers perceived a difference between the speech of older people and their own (mainly in phonology) and they tended to hypercorrect, which, according to Samuels (1989: 113), "is the same as that found by Labov in immigrant families in New York."

2.2. Bailey's model

We could affirm with Fasold (1990: 265) that "Developmental linguistics, an approach led by Charles-James Bailey, may be the most comprehensive attempt to develop a complete linguistic theory that includes variation and change". In the model proposed by Bailey time plays a paramount role since the final aim is to explain the nature of language by understanding the process

---

[66] Regarding this same idea, see the concept of social network with dense and non-dense relationships below.

that made it the way it is and, in this sense, it is intimately related to historical linguistics.

Besides diachrony, this model takes into consideration other aspects of languages: socio-communicative and neuro-biological influences. The former refer to those factors shaping a language due to its use by speakers, among which we could consider ethnic group, gender, social status and style. These are basically the same as mentioned in the Labovian model and are quantified in a very similar way. The neuro-biological aspect is related to the abilities human beings put to work when learning a language as well as to the physiological development of linguistic capacities. This neuro-biological factor is measured according to different parameters and varies from one individual to another despite the fact that the ability to use language is innate in all of us.

According to Bailey, languages tend to keep a balance between these two (social and physiological) aspects, so that the linguistic habits of a particular speaker will be determined not only by his or her socio-economic context but also by his or her physiological constitution. Thus, for example, a speaker with an impairment of the speech organs affecting his diction will have a slightly different consonantal system from other members of the same speech community, even though all of them share the same social characteristics. Labov rejects the idea of the imbalance between what is socio-communicative and what is biological since he considers them as mutually exclusive. Mutual exclusion is due to the fact that in many cases the socio-cultural factor exerts such a great pressure on the biological factor that the latter may be completely cancelled out. Thus, the dynamic model posited by Bailey considers that evidence of neuro-biological factors can be found in certain change patterns which are repeated from one language to another and which seem to be independent of any socio-communicative considerations. This approach of Bailey's may be viewed as in some ways close to Chomskyan innatism.

Another aspect in which Bailey's model clearly differs from others which address language variation is the fact that the dynamic model insists on the analysis of systems that are above the analysis of specific variation, that is to say, variation models must be included within a major system. In this way the linguistic development of an individual can be extrapolated to understand what happens in the wider sphere of language development and it can be sequenced in time in the following way: first, acquisition of the maternal language in the child; then a process of pidginisation and creolisation; finally, language death. In fact, the system would include all the lects in a language and it would not refer only to one particular speech community.

But this development is obviously not always the same. When it occurs within a linguistic system that has no contact with any other systems (which is not likely to occur) or when a change produced by hypercorrections occurs, we should speak of a development which is co-natural to the system. Another type of ab-natural change, however, is due to the (conscious) attention paid to discourse as well as to language contact and interference with other languages. So-called abnatural changes are central to my study.

In their eagerness to link purely socio-communicative and neurobiological aspects, Bailey (1987: 49) and his followers have found some evidence that the brain sends information to the speech organs in syllable sized units. This can be shown in language acquisition by observing how some sequences are harder to learn than others (as is the case of those with an initial velar and a final apical sound, since the movements of the back of the tongue are much slower than those of the apex). Notwithstanding the emphasis on phonology which is normal in variation studies, it is important to point out that Bailey's dynamic model has also been applied to morphology and word order, although it is not optimally useful for the study of borrowing as an indicator of language change and even less so for historical linguistic situations for which the quantification of any type of neuro-biological factor is out of the question.

2.3. Milroy's model

The inherent risks in an interview aimed at measuring variables according to the Labovian model made Labov himself consider that it might be more appropriate, in order to avoid interference, that the socio-cultural levels of interviewed and interviewer not be excessively different. He came to the conclusion that a member of the community should act as interviewer. From this, one can infer that there is nothing better than the observation of the relations established among subjects themselves. And this is how the social networks model proposed by James and Lesley Milroy was developed. The concept of "social network" was introduced by Radcliffe-Brown in 1940 and elaborated by Barnes (1954, 1969, 1972) and Bott (1957), to be adopted some years later by sociologists and political scientists. An illustrative definition of social network is given by Boissevain (1987: 165):

Relatives and friends, groups, and institutional complexes may be viewed partly as a scattering of points connected by lines that form a network. The points are of course persons and the lines social relations. This network of interconnected people can be seen to have a definite structure.

The network structure (recognisable in the regularities that it exhibits) has an influence on the behaviour and certain aspects of its members' personalities. In turn, the network can itself be influenced by many factors. According to Kapferer (1969), the characteristics of social networks can be grouped according to the structural criteria of interaction. Such interaction criteria are the following:

A. Multiplexity: the degree to which the relationships among people are formed by one or several chains. Boissevain (1987) provides the example of a music teacher and a pupil, who he only knows as a pupil, and this is a uniplex relation. However, if the same teacher has another pupil who is, at the same time, his nephew, his neighbour and a member of the same chamber orchestra, their relationship is "multiplex", since teacher and pupil share at least four different relations. Social anthropologists have often assumed that multiple relations provide those sharing them with more possibilities to influence on one another through one or more of the roles they play. Such situations would have been common in Scandinavian England.

B. Transactional content of the relation: the type of relations that are established. According to the analyses, we can conclude that all relationships are to a certain extent negotiated.

C. Exchange direction: most relationships are asymmetrical. In those cases in which such unbalance in the flow of goods and services is evident we can easily perceive the direction. The lack of symmetry observed indicates the difference in social level and relative power. The relation between the Scandinavian and the Anglo-Saxon communities must have been an asymmetrical one, in the sense of Thomas & Wareing (1999).

D. Frequency and duration of interaction: in those cases in which people interact more often and during longer periods there is a greater tendency for a greater exchange and for multiplex relations to appear. Therefore, considering that the Scandinavian presence is the result of immigration and not of the random settlement of a small number of warriors, there would be multiplex relations among the members of a given community, despite the fact that they belonged to different ethnic groups (Anglo-Saxons and Scandinavians). They fulfil the two conditions of maintaining frequent relations over a long period of time.

Besides these four interaction criteria there are also some others of a structural nature which may be used for the analysis of a particular network:

A. Size of the network: there is an area we could call the first level, formed by the person's direct contacts. This same person can also be introduced to others of his/her direct contacts' acquaintances. These "friends of friends" are also important since they are accessible and because we can evaluate the members of an individual's network in terms of the number and quality of the relations they, in turn, establish with the people making decisions in their community. In this sense, the men belonging to the jury (see chapter three, above) may be important because as witness to commercial transactions they belong to the second level area and, at the same time, they establish more than one relationship with the tradesmen: as neighbour and as representative of the law.

B. Density of the network: degree to which the members of a speaker's network, independently from him, are in contact. The density of a network can be calculated with a formula expressing the proportion between the total number of possible relations and those which in fact occur. Generally speaking, when a network's density is high there is a considerable degree of social communication and, therefore, greater pressure on the individual speaker to adapt to current linguistic uses. In the case of the communities under study here it is not possible to apply this formula, since we cannot have access to data on those communities' populations. In Coates' opinion, when networks are relatively dense they function as norm-enforcement mechanisms, that is, "closely-knit groups will have the capacity to enforce linguistic norms" (1986: 80). Conversely, tightly-knit networks are mechanisms for language maintenance. So perhaps medieval English communities were more open, thus favouring language change.

C. Centrality: it is an index of the accessibility of a particular member regarding others in the same network. The more central an individual is, the bigger his/her capacity to establish communication, or to influence or manipulate it. Thus, a high degree of centrality is, in principle, a source of power.[67] This conclusion is entirely consistent with Labov's (1984) finding that innovating groups are located centrally in class structure (Milroy and Milroy 1992).

D. The level at which the members of a network form small groups whose members have a tighter relation between them than with the rest of the individuals in the network: if one person perceives the existence of these groups, he or she will modify his behaviour, since such groups tend to create certain norms that exert pressure on individuals. This accounts for the difficulty of belonging to two groups with different norms at the same time.

Besides the objective structural and interaction criteria, a set of subjective criteria there exists determining the different areas in a network around an individual and constantly fluctuating. Differences from one network to the other are increased by basic factors such as biological ones (sex, age, etc.)[68], the community, social influences and personality.

There is no doubt that an analysis based on social networks may provide a systematic basis for the study of the tension and assimilation of social relationships. Likewise, it provides a means to relate formal abstract sociological analyses with everyday experience, since it links personal relations and institutions or power.

As regards language change, one of the reasons that it occurs is the influence of elements from outside the community (either speakers of a different language or of the same language with different rules). Since strong social networks (high density) are mechanisms favouring the norm, any influence from outside the community must reach it by means of people who have been accepted in it, given that its networks must be open enough to accept the influences of other, different networks (from other speech communities). I think this is the case of Scandinavian England: had the newcomers not been accepted in the places where they settled, there would have been a great deal

---

67 Boissevain (1987: 166) explains this concept as follows: "A person who lives in a centrally located house is able to see his friends more often and thus, usually, is better informed than people who live far away from 'the centre of things'. Just what 'the centre of things' is, depends on the nature of the problem being examined".

68 Age and sex are regarded as social factors by Labov and as neuro-biological by Bailey.

less contact between both languages, and it would not have fostered changes in English (at least in its lexicon) to the degree observed.

3. Speech community

All the models above mention the term "speech community", although none of them provides a universally valid definition. The concept of speech community has been considered essential by many authors (Fasold 1990) and, notwithstanding this, has often gone undefined. It is generally used to classify speakers according to strict linguistic criteria, and in some contexts the concepts "speech community" and "domain" have been felt to be equivalent. In Mioni's (1987: 170) words, a domain is:

> ...theoretical construct that designates a cluster of interaction situation, if grouped around the same field of experience, and tied together by a shared range of goals and obligations: e.g. family, neighbourhood, religion, work, etc. The domains which are relevant in a given community classify speech acts and events into classes of sociolinguistic situations whose components are congruent between them and are usually accompanied by the appropriate language/variety.

Clearly, it is difficult to find a definition of speech community where linguistic regulations are so different from one social group to another, as Fasold (1990: 41) proposes. If, following Fasold, we consider that what is important about a speech community is not that a particular language variety is shared, but that language regulations are shared, we can also agree with Saville-Troike's (1982: 20) definition of speech community. From the standpoint of the ethnography of communication, she affirms that one individual may belong to more than one speech community at the same time, perhaps in a similar way that he may be a member of more than one social network.

From this point of view, we can consider that a speaker of Scandinavian origin established in England may have the same regulations when speaking than an Anglo-Saxon native, although their language varieties are not the same. In fact, due to his occupation this hypothetical speaker may be a member of a social network whose other members are Anglo-Saxons (let us think, for example, of any tradesman or craftsman established in an urban community who must necessarily interact and communicate with his neighbours) and would belong, therefore, to a speech community that coincides with that social network. At the same time, the same speaker may have some direct contact with other people of Scandinavian descent in neighbouring villages who, in turn, belong to another network and speech community. As can be seen, the concept of "speech community is a slippery one and it is intimately related in cases such as these to the phenomenon of language contact.

4. Language contact

When Weinreich began exploring the field of language contact at the beginning of the 1950's, one of his proposals (1953: 1) was not to make any difference as to whether the contact occurred among speakers of different languages, dialects of a single language or variants within a single dialect. In the same vein, Oksaar (1974: 491) provides the study of the phenomenon with its present sociolinguistic character:

> ...the social, economic and cultural environment in which the contact of languages and integration of linguistic innovations takes place is of vital importance for our understanding of the whole process, and its role must not only be stressed, but also taken into actual consideration in future studies.

Although researchers over the last decades always mention the importance of the socio-cultural context of speakers when dealing with language contact, only a few have referred to it in any depth. Thus, Giles and Smith (1979), drawing on Psycholinguistics, they build their theory on "speech accommodation". Accordingly, speakers can adapt to one another (convergence), they can create distance between one another (divergence), and can also keep their own use of the code. According to Giles, interlocutors adapt to each other depending on the relation between them and their own view of that relation: this is the basis both for code selection and for any later code (language) shifting.

Haugen also dealt with language contact and established a direct relation between it and language change. Haugen (1980: 152) claims that the speed of evolution depends on "the deliberate will of a group to do so. But this can only occur if the development is perceived as a problem calling for a solution". Only two years earlier he had stated that not all the elements in the lexical system of a language are equally stable in a contact situation but that non-primary words are more easily introduced than those referring to the subsistence of everyday life (Haugen 1978: 36). In the current study, I have observed that the lexical field where the highest number of Scandinavian loanwords has been recorded is that of terms referring to everyday life, small household objects, etc. (which I have labelled 12 in Chapter Four).

Van Coetsem's (1987) consideration goes a little further, once one has accepted that the issue is essentially part of the study of borrowing (already anticipated by Moravscik 1978: 110-ff). He also believes there is always both a source and a target language[69], and distinguishes (Van Coetsem 1987: 51) between the speaker of the target and source language whenever he is dealing with contact situations. This leads him to mention the following differences:

> If the recipient language speaker is the agent, as is the case of the English speaker using French words while speaking English, the transfer of material (...) from the source language to the recipient language is borrowing. If, on the other hand, the source language speaker is the agent, as is the case of a French-speaker using his French articulatory habits while speaking English, the transfer of material from the source language to the recipient language is *imposition*.

He concludes that if the speaker of the recipient language is the agent, he will tend to keep his phonological system, whereas he may accept some elements from the source language vocabulary. This is due to the fact that, in general, the phonological system of any language is considered more stable than its lexical system. We can also infer that the transfer from one source language to a recipient language affects, in the first place, those spheres that are less stable, especially vocabulary in the case of borrowing, and those more stable spheres (phonological entities in particular) in the case of imposition (Geerts 1987: 604). However, we cannot consider that all the elements in the lexical system of a given language have a uniform degree of stability (Haugen 1967: 93-ff). There is, then, a gradient regarding stability not only from one system to the other but also within each.

In the particular case of Anglo-Scandinavian or Anglo-Norse, this phenomenon is found to operate on a twofold dimension. Taking Old Norse dialects brought to England to be the source language, and late Old English (in its different diatopic varieties) the recipient language, we can see how borrowing occurs when the agent in the communication is the speaker of the recipient language. In other words, when the Anglo-Saxon speaker uses Scandinavian terms in his conversation, a process of borrowing is taking place. If the speaker of the source language (in our case, any variety of Old Norse)

---

69   Weinreich (1953: 31) refers to "source language" and "recipient language".

used his pronunciation scheme to pronounce English words, this would be a case of imposition. Both phenomena occurred in Scandinavian England. There is clear evidence of Scandinavian loanwords in English. It might have been the native speakers of English who developed this process within their language. Yet at the same time, we can observe the imposition of certain Scandinavian phonological features upon the recipient language (English) during the Middle English period, due to the articulatory habits of the Scandinavians who, once settled in the Isles, began to use English with their own pronunciation. Thus can we explain how the grapheme <g> + front vowel ceased to be pronounced as /j/ and became the velar plosive which we pronounce in words where Chaucer pronounced a palatal (*give*). Similarly, the palatal realisation of <c> as it appears in OE *circe* is transformed into the velar plosive that we can still hear in certain Northern and Eastern areas of England and Scotland, as in the place-name suffix *-kirk* (Fellows-Jensen 1987).

There are also some cases of simultaneous imposition and borrowing. The OE word *scirt* was pronounced with an initial palatal and was used to refer to a particular item of clothing, probably something short. At the same time ON had a feminine noun, *skyrta*, that meant something similar to "coat" and which was pronounced with initial /sk/. Both terms survived in English, but with both their form and meaning modified, so that we nowadays have *shirt* (with its typical Anglo-Saxon palatal) and *skirt* (with its Scandinavian pronunciation) and both with different extra-linguistic referents in a clear case of semantic change (Moskowich 2005a).

It should be borne in mind that this process of contact suggests different phenomena if we consider it from a broader perspective: variation, diglossia, bilingualism, language conflict, code switching, language shift and creolisation. From the perspective of the individual speaker this is reflected in interference, transference, borrowing, substitution, integration, etc. The different situations thus arising are essentially bilingualism and diglossia, as well as the birth of creoles, as we will see in what follows.

5. Bilingualism and diglossia

Language is the result of life in society. According to Hymes (1972: 5): "The role of a language is relative to the place of that language, or way of speaking, the history and repertoire of a community. Here, as generally, structure depends upon function: the significance of features of language cannot be assessed without knowledge of their social matrix."

Labov (1972) referred to it in the following terms: "Language is a form of social behavior, it is used by humans in a social context, communicating their needs, emotions and ideas to one another". But it often happens that we find more than one language or language variety in the same social system, and it is in such contact situations that the phenomena mentioned above evolve.

During the first half of the twentieth century linguistic study has tried to discover the structure of languages, looking at their systems of reference and representation, often to the exclusion of any other approach. However, from the 1980s great importance has been attached to the social component inherent to languages. In fact, contact phenomena cannot be explained on the grounds of language structure alone. I agree with Iglesias Rábade (1986), and with the approach of Sociolinguistics in general, in the criticism of Chomsky's (1965: 3) position:

> Linguistic theory is concerned primarily with an ideal speaker-listener in a completely homogeneous speech-community, who knows its language perfectly, and is unaffected by such grammatically irrelevant conditions as memory limitations, distractions, shifts of attention and interest, and errors (random or characteristic) in applying his knowledge in actual performance.

That is, the definition of speech community seems to have been avoided in linguistics, so that what might be at the least an uncomfortable situation be in turn avoided.

Once the idea that the structural dimension of language is the only instrument for its study has been rejected, we turn to the functional one "that is, descriptive of its social uses in communication. Since the study of linguistic structure is regarded by linguists as their central task, it remains for sociolinguists to devote themselves to the study of the functional problem" (Haugen 1971: 103).

A community shares regulations and norms concerning the structure of a language, style and language production (Labov 1972). When speakers share a common socio-cultural context and communicate by means of a more or less standardised code which is valid for all functions, such norms are unconsciously respected. But sometimes they are consciously followed through different forms of agreement with contextual stimuli, thus favouring different variants created by different sub-groups (or sub-speech communities) associated with certain social strata dissatisfied with the dominant values.

Although it is extremely difficult to define bilingualism (Pap 1982; Mackey 1987), given that it may refer to a characteristic of individual speakers or to the social group, it may be regarded as competence in two languages or in two varieties of the same language, etc., and some authors have tried to provide a concise explanation. Bloomfield (1933) defined it as "a native-like control of two languages". Haugen (1953: 7), also from the point of view of the individual speaker, refers to the ability "to produce complete and meaningful utterances in the other language". However, Haugen goes on to mention (1956: 10) two dimensions when dealing with bilingualism: "The speaker's knowledge of each language, which may range from a mere smattering to literary mastery, and b) the language distance, ranging from a barely perceptible difference to completely contrasting structures."

Up to this point, then, the two main ways to interpret bilingualism are either as the superficial knowledge of two languages or as a literary competence in the non-native tongue. Many linguists seem to believe it is an individual phenomenon. Fishman (1972: 129), for example, affirms that "bilingualism is essentially a characterisation of individual linguistic versatility". In the same vein, researchers such as Ninyoles (1977: 220-221) claim that "el bilingüismo es una situación propia del comportamiento lingüístico individual... en el bilingüismo las dos variedades lingüísticas cumplen las mismas funciones, es decir, pueden ser usadas en una sociedad tanto para la comunicación formal como para las relaciones no formales".

Theodor W. Elwert (1973: 1) distinguishes, in turn, three basic types of bilingualism in an approach which even at the time was somewhat old-fashioned:

1) individual bilingualism: a speaker acquires a "native-like control of two or more languages".
2) social bilingualism: most individuals in particular a geographical or social area speak two languages.
3) stylistic bilingualism: one same groups speaks two forms of the same language for different purposes (in other words, there is a functional difference).

Badía's definition (1977: 111) is also worth mentioning here, because in restricting bilingualism to the sphere of the individual he takes into consideration the speaker's context, claiming that "tales personas han aprendido la realidad en su momento (es decir, la niñez) por medio de dos lenguas al mismo tiempo".

In his study of the linguistic situation of Norman and Plantagenet England, Iglesias Rábade (1992: 145-ff) reformulates some of his previous positions (1986) and establishes eight types of linguistic behaviour applied to both the individual and the collective levels. To this end, he takes into consideration the speaker's competence in the different varieties of the two languages in contact (L1 and L2), colloquial or A (the linguistic habits resulting from a primary and basic, natural and cumulative process) and learned or B (the result of a secondary cultural addition to the basic form). L1 is defined as a native language which is related to a particular geographical area for historical reasons, whereas L2 is the upstart language which coincides in the same area as the L1 due to some structural imposition on the native society. The eight types of linguistic behaviour that can be found in contact situations at an individual level are:

1) L1A: Limited speakers who only know the A variety of the native language and are not competent in its high variety. Iglesias Rábade calls these "primary monoglots" or "natural monolinguals". This situation occurs in England after the Scandinavian colonisation only in places which, due to the remoteness of their location, have no contact with the newcomers. This could have happened in the southwest. Besides, it would apply only to the members of the lowest ranks of Anglo-Saxon society, such as *gebur*, *geneat* and *cotsetla*, whose lives were bond to agricultural production and who had no relation with speakers from different social strata. Their relationships with the nobility or the clergy was merely official (payment of taxes, performance of rite) and did not necessarily imply linguistic intercourse.

2) L1AB: Individuals who know both varieties of their mother tongue. Iglesias Rábade labels these "secondary monoglots" or "educated monolinguals". This is the type of linguistic behaviour present in members of the clergy and perhaps some other men who could read and write (a rather infrequent situation in a mostly illiterate society).

3) L1AB + L2A: Speakers with a competence in both varieties of their native language and the colloquial one of the non-native one. Such speakers are "balanced bilinguals". This is the situation typical of Scandinavian England, mainly in the regions inhabited by Scandinavians, like the Danelaw and the Territory of the Five Boroughs, where it is very likely that Anglo-Saxons were able to communicate with the Norse and Danish peasants working with them in the fields under the same lord or, where on meeting at the market place they were able to make commercial transactions or converse about the weather and crops.

4) L1AB + L2B: Individuals who are competent in the two varieties of their mother tongue as well as in the high variety of the non-native language. These are "balanced bilinguals". In the Anglo-Scandinavian case, this phenomenon is more important than is generally ackowledged. Traditionally, the Scandinavian terms taken into English were said to be related to everyday life (that is to say, belonging to the colloquial variety of ON) and only a few terms of a technical character (that is, pertaining to the high variety) were adopted. However, I have been able to trace a larger number of technical Scandinavian terms in ME than might *a priori* be considered, although it is true they are so incardinated in the language that they often do not appear in texts of a technical character (Iglesias Rábade and Moskowich 1997).

5) L1A + L2AB: Individuals who have only acquired the colloquial variety of their mother tongue but are competent in both varieties of the upstart language. These are "diglossic bilinguals" according to Iglesias Rábade (1992: 148): "En realidad, impedimentos de tipo social (prejuicios, autoodio, etc.) inclinan a ciertos hablantes al desconocimiento deliberado de la variedad culta de su lengua materna y nativa, y buscan en la lengua advenediza el complemento necesario para la comunicación formal."

There is no evidence that this type of linguistic behaviour may have been present in Scandinavian England, perhaps because the newcomers integrated into the Anglo-Saxon society to a higher degree than was formerly thought, so that there was strong functional motivation for their acquisition of the high variety of Old Norse in that it helped them to climb the social ladder.

6) L1A + L2A: Speakers who only know the colloquial varieties of both languages. These are usually individuals who speak their mother tongue in the only variety they acquired as children and progressively learned the colloquial variety of the non-native language. Also in this group may be children acquiring both languages at the same time without reaching the competence in the B variety of either. This type of speaker is a "primary or natural semibilingual". This, arguably, is the most abundant type of speaker in England after the arrival of the Scandinavian migrants, especially in the Danelaw area. Both options probably existed. Let us take the case of a grown-up speaker, an Anglo-Saxon peasant competent in L1A, who, due to his social origins, does not know the educated or high variety of his mother tongue. He may have established some relationship with a Danish or Norse family in the neighbourhood and have learned the rudiments of the low variety of Old Norse. If we extend our example a little further, we can imagine that he might marry the daughter of a Norse family. Their children would also be natural or primary semibilinguals (but acquiring both languages at the same time). Another situation that might have existed, and that perfectly fits into this type of linguistic behaviour, is the case of the *gerefa* (cf. chapter two). On the one hand, this officer had to communicate with his lord (be he Anglo-Saxon or Scandinavian) and would have done so in a single language. On the other hand, he also had to transmit certain directions to the lord's workers, who might have been Anglo-Saxon or Danish, and would therefore have needed to speak both languages or at least to be able to be understood by all, despite any lexical and phonological peculiarities in his speech.
7) L1A + L2B: Individuals who are competent in the colloquial variety of their mother tongue and in the high variety of the non-native language, called "diglossic semibilinguals". It is difficult to find this type of phenomena in Anglo-Scandinavian England since it is generally found in decontextualised language learning and this is not typically the case of languages sharing the same physical space.
8) L1AB + L2AB: According to this scheme, it would be difficult to find a speaker who is competent in both varieties (colloquial and educated) of both languages. According to Iglesias Rábade (1992: 150), from an individual perspective, this speaker is "ambibilingual" because he is fa-

miliar with the absolute potentialities of both languages. However, he adds:

> Es el bilingüismo perfecto que sólo puede darse en ciertos individuos de cualidades muy singulares, por tanto *en el plano colectivo*, se trata de un planteamiento lingüístico utópico, aunque es frecuente en nuestros días que las autoridades de la lengua "superior" se empeñen en demostrar su viabilidad.

It is highly unlikely that such a speaker could have existed unless he was some kind of erudite monk (as in the example proposed by Iglesias Rábade himself) or a *skáldr* able to compose his verses in both languages and, at the same time, to communicate with his Danish and English audience (maybe not a very learned one). In fact, it is hard to believe that speakers beyond puberty could ever acquire a native-like competence when learning a second language (Birdsong 1992; Flege and Yeni-Komshian 1999).

As regards collective linguistic behaviour, it is clear that fewer can be established:

1) L1A: This is a speech community that preserves its vernacular (here opposed to standard, as balanced development of both A y B varieties). This occurs when a language does not develop its high or learned variety because the functions for which it would be used are already performed by another language. This is the situation of Norman England when French or Anglo-Norman replaced learned English. However, it is unlikely that this same situation occurred before the Conquest. There are various reasons for this, among them the fact that there is no evidence of a political or cultural superiority on the part of the Scandinavian colonisers.

2) L1AB: A collective situation like this is again difficult to conceive for historical and social, rather than to linguistic, reasons. That all the members of a community knew both varieties of their language is not really believable, especially when we consider that most communities were rural ones.

3) L1AB + L2A: As in the previous case, it is not feasible that a whole community is competent in both varieties of the vernacular and, at the same time, in the colloquial variety of the non-native language. This may have occurred, however, at an individual level as exemplified above.

4) L1AB + L2B: At a collective level this is a rather infrequent situation in language contact settings. It is not conceivable that native Anglo-Saxons would learn the high variety of Old Norse, except perhaps some literary formulae to be found in the sagas, since scaldic poetry was much less widespread.
5) L1A + L2AB: This diglossic bilingualism is quite often found in collective linguistic behaviour when speakers "por razones de tipo social consideran el uso de la lengua nativa inadecuado e incluso irrespetuoso para una situación formal, precisamente porque se vincula secularmente al hablante de la lengua nativa con una clase social también secularmente proscrita" (Iglesias Rabáde 1992: 148). However, this is far from being the situation of Scandinavian England, where no stigmatisation in the use of Old or Middle English high varieties seems to have taken place.
6) L1A + L2A: This behaviour is considered one of the most widespread, mainly in cases such as that which interests us here, in which two communities share two languages and have a low degree of literacy. It could be argued that this type of situation was not only the most common one in Norman England but also in the period immediately preceding it. We may think of a situation in which two speakers communicate, and try to get closer to each in other's language. This mutual movement (convergence) would appear essentially in survival-related spheres (trade, agriculture, etc.). Any attempt of self-assertion on the part of either of the two speakers would be excluded, since the fact that one was speaking either Old Norse or Old English would suppose no kind of social "mark" at all (exactly the opposite than an Anglo-Norman context).
7) L1A + L2B: This behaviour, typical of decontextualised second language acquisition, is more abundant nowadays than in the Middle Ages. In fact, in the period under survey here we cannot really imagine linguistic behaviour with these characteristics since languages were learned *in situ*, even in the case of Latin, used in monasteries for real communication.
8) L1AB + L2AB: This model was not present either in a collective or any other societal level and appears only seldom in individual speakers.

The term "diglossia" has been mentioned in some of the linguistic patterns described above, and it certainly deserves some comment here, since it has been debated and modified since being first used by Charles A. Ferguson. His definition is as follows (1959: 36):

> a relatively stable language situation in which, in addition to the primary dialects of the language (which may include a standard or regional standards) there is a very divergent, highly codified (often grammatically more complex) superposed variety, the vehicle of a large and respected body of written literature, either of an early period or in another speech community, which is learned largely by formal education and is used for most written and formal purposes but is not used by any other sector of the community for ordinary conversation[70].

According to this definition such a situation is absolutely usual for any speaker of any language, since he will tend to use one variety or the other depending on the situation and contact he is in, according to whether a more or less formal variety of the language is required.

Fishman (1967) further develops this idea, looking at the case of a social group, using not two varieties of the same language, but two different languages for the same functions as a high (for formal situations) and a low (informal situations) variety would be used respectively. Considering all related factors, Fishman developed four different characterisations of diglossia and bilingualism: bilingualism with and without diglossia; diglossia with and without bilingualism.

1) Bilingualism with diglossia appears in those speech communities in which speakers play different social roles; the access to such roles is favoured by institutions and they have clearly different functions and uses.
2) Bilingualism without diglossia implies the existence and use of two different linguistic codes for all and the same functions. This would be a non-economical situation. With no different functions for each of the two languages, the situation would be felt to be superfluous and would probably disappear.
3) Diglossia without bilingualism is the use of two varieties of the same language with a clear social difference.

---

70 In his 1991 article "Diglossia revisited" Ferguson himself reconsiders many of the approaches to the term and the language situation underpinning it.

4) Neither bilingualism nor diglossia: this could be found in an extremely small and isolated community and is, as such, a completely hypothetical setting.

6. Pidgins and creoles

Language contact, as we are beginning to see, has many different outcomes. Among these are pidgin and creoles, which are usually dealt with together in the literature. This may be due to the fact that the earliest researchers here hardly ever established a distinction between the terms. Both imply, from the point of view of structure, great variability and quick-paced change, and both tend to appear in multilingual contexts. However, not all contact situations result in creoles (Görlach 1990, 1992). Considering their typological affinities, we can say that neither pidgins nor creoles have an inflected morphology whereas both display identical aspectual systems and the same word-order pattern (SVO).

From a social point of view, they tend not to be viewed positively either by their own speakers (where they are language-conscious) or by the speakers of the corresponding superstratum languages (in fact they were not officially recognised by governments until the late 1960s). They were considered incorrect linguistic systems because the recipients (whose mother tongue was the subordinate one) belonged to such a low cultural level that there was no way they could understand a "correct" message in the superordinate language. Thus, for a long time the following explanation, by Bloomfield (1933: 472), was accepted as valid:

> Speakers of a lower language may make so little progress in learning the dominant speech, that the masters, in communicating with them resort to 'baby-talk'. This 'baby-talk' is the master's imitation of the subjects' incorrect speech. There is no reason to believe that it is by no means an exact imitation, and that some of its features are based not upon the subjects' mistakes but upon grammatical relations that exist within the upper language itself. The subject, in turn, deprived of the correct model, can do no better now than to acquire the simplified 'baby-talk' version of the upper language.

In more recent times such descriptions have been roundly disproved by generativists and others. Bickerton (1981: 4), for instance, claims that in order for a creole to appear, social intercourse must be maintained constant[71]. Creoles develop from pidgins that have existed for no longer than a generation and often in populations where around 20% are speakers of a native language or languages, with the other 80% constituting different linguistic groups. This idea can be further discussed basing on the choice of language-external conditions since they are not met in a certain number of cases (Mülhäusler 1987: 650).

One of the most striking characteristics of pidgins is their lack of linguistic continuation, which itself reflects the lack of continuation of the societies in which they emerge. As a general rule such societies witness more sudden changes and upheavals and less gradual development than other societies. In this sense, we can concur with Bailey (1973) and Domingue (1977) that Middle English is a creole (or "hybrid" language) originating in the contact of different languages. In fact, the main difference any non expert reader may find between a text in Middle English (which he can more or less understand) and one in Old English is, according to Domingue (1977: 90), more a matter of language-external than language-internal factors, since "the internal approach does not account for the rapidity of the implementation of changes and does not take note of the era during which they occurred". Contact with Old Norse is one of the external factors that may have accelerated or even provoked processes such as the reduction of inflections and the subsequent more rigid word-order. Such an idea was first mentioned by Bailey and Maroldt (1977), although in reference to a French rather than to a Scandinavian-based creole, and is later supported by Poussa (1982) and Görlach (1992). In fact, many other authors (Bailey & Maroldt 1977; Percy 1991; Hickey 2002; McWhorter 2002; Pintzuk 2002) have dealt with the loss of morphological endings in Middle English in the same way. Other authors, however, reject the creolisation hypothesis for English (Dalton-Puffer 1995; Danchev 1997; Dawson 2003).

In Iglesias Rábade's (1992: 141) approach pidgins represent an extreme case of bilingual borrowing since what is borrowed is the whole language with all its sub-systems (grammatical, phonemic and lexical). However, the speech community initiating this massive borrowing process mutilates many of the basic grammatical structures of the language under pidginisation. This

---

71 By enhancing the importance of psychological prerequisites for language acquisition, the author is directly referring to Generativism.

gives rise to a particular language state that, one might argue, cannot be extended to the whole community, but only to certain sectors. It is difficult to demonstrate to what an extent the same happened in the period prior to the Norman Conquest, due to the lack of records. Nevertheless, accepting that this type of process happened is perhaps better than looking for stylistic reasons for the introduction of certain innovations in the language. Indeed, stylistic motivations can be disregarded in our context, since using Old Norse loanwords did not imply any special elegance or glamour, with relationships between Scandinavians and Anglo-Saxons more symmetrical than those between the Anglo-Saxons and the Normans, which carried an evident social imbalance (although I do not mean that the Scandinavians were not prestigious). No doubt a certain degree of pidginisation of Old English and Old Norse occurred as a result of relations between these communities.

Shippey (1986) exemplifies what could have happened to the inflectional system of Old English, using the following well-known reconstructed situation: two Danelaw farmers are involved in the transaction of a horse. One of them is of Anglo-Saxon descent and the other was born in a Danish family. Both understand that the object of the transaction is a horse since word bases are similar and mutually intelligible (ON *hross* and OE *hors*). The problem appears when adding inflectional endings or any other linguistic material to that base. In Shippey's example the problem arises when adding the determiner, in that it behaves so differently in Old English and Old Norse. In Old Norse, the determiner is usually an enclitic form following the noun (Dan. *bilet* vs. PE *the car*; Dan. *bogen* vs. PE *the book*). Similarly, these two tenth-century farmers could not easily know how many horses were involved in the conversation if one said OE *þæt hors* and the other ON *hrossit* since they could only understand the word's root. According to this theory, which is supported by other authors (Leith 1947; Romaine 1988, etc.), the easiest solution was to leave endings aside and favour those parts of lexemes that were largely understood by most speakers of both languages. There is evidence that the case of Scandinavian loans in English is unusual since not only lexical elements, but grammatical formations and function words are also borrowed (Herbert 2007). Authors such as Kerswill (2002) deal with situations like these as cases of *köineisation* both in the regional population (speakers of Old English and early Middle English) and with immigrants (speakers of Old Norse).

7. A brief overview of lexical change

Since this study uses a lexical corpus it seems necessary to mention some basic aspects of the lexico-semantic system of English. Although we are dealing here with borrowing, there is also the possibility that semantic change might occur, with the meaning of an already existing form undergoing a shift due to interference from other languages. Of course, the meaning of "meaning" is difficult to define and is one of the most ambiguous and controversial terms in linguistic theory. The controversy between the realists and the nominalists has been a long one. As early as 1916 Saussure, from an idealist perspective, proposes a dual conception of the sign in which the meaning, the signified, is the mental image evoked by the signifier. That is, he conceives of meanings as conventional and arbitrary relations between signs and extralinguistic realities. Other authors such as Kronasser (1952) follow along similar lines.

After this binary conception, a more complex one emerges. Ogden and Richards (1923) propose a semiotic triangle or triadic model of the sign according to which we can consider, a) the conceptual representation, b) the linguistic body of the word for designating one particular extralinguistic object, and c) the extralinguistic object itself. Later definitions, such as those of Bloomfield (1933: 21) and Lyons (1968, 1981), have specified elements that form part of the signified but, generally speaking, these and other definitions, like Leith's (1947: 70-73), conclude that meanings, the signified, have the following elements:

1. A relationship of a sign's material structure, either phonetically or graphically manifested.
2. Certain psychological factors typical of the speaker.
3. A reference to extralinguistic elements.

When any of these three factors is altered a new term for an already existing referent will be introduced. This is the case with the substitution of OE *niman* by ME *taken* (de ON *taka*). Another possible consequence of altering one of the above three factors is that an already existing form is now used to refer to a different referent, as in ON *bread* and OE *hlaf*. More recently, it has been claimed that in linguistic substitution (including lexical substitution) a complete process "of bilinguation" must have occurred, with speakers abandoning their L1 in order to communicate with their children (Bastardas Boada 2006:

25). Massive bilingualism may have led to lexical substitution in Middle English.

It is in the lexicon that language change is most easily detected. The causes and nature of lexical change are more clearly delimited than those for phonological or syntactic change. In fact, it seems that part of present-day English has specific cultural origins, identified through historical studies that do not apply to other linguistic structures. Conversely, it is difficult to establish precise laws for lexical change, whereas changes in the sound system are not difficult to express in such terms.

From the early days of Semantics writers tried to list the main motivations favouring change. Such motivations were: a) discontinuity in the transmission of languages from one generation to the following one; b) loss of motivation, which dissociates a word from its origins and sets it on a new journey; c) the vagueness of a word's meaning that can be adapted to different semantic situations; d) a speech community's cultural development that makes it slowly change its habits, institutions, or that is subject to the imposition of an alien culture; e) the psychological state of many of its speakers, who discover new metaphors, meaning associations that appear little by little and spread in the speech community; f) taboos, leading to speakers substituting other terms.

Meillet (1965: 230-271) proposes three other causes for semantic change: a change in the context in which certain terms appear (if the usual context of a word is altered, the meaning can be modified), change in reference (mentioned above when referring to taboos) and change produced by the relationships among the different social groups (certain socio-historical events have a definitive influence on changes in meaning).

Lehmann (1973) in turn classifies semantic change in a different way:

1: Context reduction. When a word's context is reduced it tends to survive with a very restricted meaning, or preserving some archaic meaning. This is what happens with PE *ghost* whose primary meaning is not the same as in the restricted context *Holy Ghost*.
2: Context expansion. Words that initially had a clearly defined meaning and later spread to many contexts. ModE *picture* had a limited meaning, referring to paintings, but in PE this meaning has been expanded to "photograph" as well.

3: Context alteration. This is normally caused by the influence of geographical, technical or social dialects. Sometimes the new meaning pushes the original one and, if so, we must think that this is due to social prejudices. In this way, *ceorl* meant "boy, mainly from the country" but the meaning of PE *churl* has clearly undergone a process of pejoration[72].

---

72 For a more detailed account of semantic change at work in the history of English see, Crespo (forthcoming) *A semantic Approach to the History of English.*

Chapter Four

The corpus

1. Plan and method

As stated above, the corpus of data for the present analysis has been extracted from the *Middle English Dictionary* edited by Hans Kurath. Publication of the dictionary began in 1956, and from 1963 onwards the team was directed by Sherman M. Kuhn, Robert E. Lewis and others. The new paper edition (1984-) adds new texts and records to the original 1956 corpus and also modifies the dating criteria and entries by the use of abbreviated titles and stencils. Three types of entries are added: those that had not been included in the 1956 edition and those published later than that; entries for editions that the team considered to be better; and some modification of stencils since 1956.

All the terms under <a>, <b> and <c> and their corresponding entries constitute the records for my corpus. I am conscious that the fact of not including entries beginning with <f> (with forms such as *fra*) and <k>, or those words with initial <sk> (most of which are of Scandinavian origin), seems to limit the number of records in the data available. The samples in the entries amount to 100,000 words and have been sorted into 5,295 different records. The database includes the following fields:

FORM: includes the form itself as well as its possible spelling variants as they are in the *MED*.
CONSTRUCTION: whenever there is one, it includes the typical construction or collocation in which it may be found in texts.
ETYMOLOGY: includes the information offered by the *MED* under this same epigraph.
ACCEPTION: includes the different meanings depending on the loanword. Meanings have been provided and recorded as stated in Section 2 of the present chapter.
SEMANTIC FIELD: a particular number key has been assigned to this field depending to the code detailed in Section 8.
GRAMMATICAL CATEGORY: each term is classified under a category following the editor's criteria (see Section 5).

INITIAL DATE: first known date for the text from which the term was extracted. As explained in Section 3, not all dates are exact and there may be a difference of twenty-five years.

AUTHOR: includes the name of the author of the text where the Scandinavian term appears. Clearly, in most cases this field remains empty since only seldom is the author known, especially in the case of legal documents.

TEXT: in this field I provide the text containing the loanword. All references have been taken as they were in the *MED*. The information concerning stanza, verse, folio, page or paragraph have been included in a separate field. The reason for using separate fields for this information is to speed up the indexing of the database.

QUOTATION: includes the particular example where the Scandinavism can be found.

BJØRKMAN YES: this is the only "logical" (yes/no) field in the database. It allows us to calculate how many of the terms (and uses) that I have selected had already been gathered by Eilert Bjørkman (1900-1902). The fact that I am using this very old work as a point of reference is because it seems to be the only one including a more or less complete list of the terms of Scandinavian origin that are otherwise scattered in the literature.

DIALECT: a three-letter key has been entered to represent the dialectal area to which the text containing the loan belongs. Two criteria have been used for classification here: first, the one established by the team compiling the *MED* from 1984 as explained in Section 7 below; second, and for those cases in which no information regarding the dialectal variety of the text was provided, such texts were ascribed to the dialect proposed by the *Early English Text Society* edition. Even after this process, there are a number of cases in which I have not been able to include this sort of information on reliable grounds, and these are the cases in which the terms do not appear in contemporary works but in articles or later studies, as with those by Ekwall (1937, 1963), the publications of the *English Place Name Society*, and any other type of association or research group. Likewise, the terms that are not marked as belonging to any particular dialect have been grouped as standard.

TEXT TYPE: field in which texts have been grouped according both to formal and content-related factors under twelve different keys. Since these keys will appear in some of the illustrative graphs and figures provided in the following pages, it may be useful to be familiar with them now:

POE: includes all non-religious poetry except for works that, although being poetic, have other content, such as legends or romances.

FIC: fiction (tales) and legends.

COS: texts containing habits and customary uses, morals and social games.

POL: includes any text referring to social organisation and political life (also criticisms and satires).

REC: includes the different versions of *Domesday Book* and *Anglo-Saxon Chronicle*, as well as records, letters, minutes, deeds and historiographical works.

TEC: technical texts (directions for the use of utensils, manuals concerning sports, hunting, navigation, astronomy, etc.). I have only excluded from this type of text those dealing with medicine and remedies (MED) and cooking recipes (COC), since these merit a group of their own given that there are a great many of them and that they could somehow modify our final results.

ROM: romances.

LIS: dictionaries, glossaries and vocabularies.

DRA: drama and theatrical plays in general.

DID: works of a didactic character, inevitably full of religious and moral references. I have also considered here all sorts of other religious texts including poetry, fragments of the Bible, hagiographies, etc., given the difficulty entailed in separating religious affairs from others in the Middle Ages.

MXT: all texts which are not easily included in any of the former groups. On many occasions, these are only a few lines contained in volumes including very different types of documents (cartularies), theatre plays, poetry or even legal records.

2. Meanings

The meanings of those forms considered to be Scandinavian loans acquire great importance, given that they are from a dictionary. As Kurath himself explains in his introduction to the *MED* (1956: 3), several types of quotations have been used to identify meanings:

a. those containing an explicit definition made by a medieval author, without taking into consideration its validity or its acceptance on the part of his contemporaries.

b. those containing synonyms and antonyms.
c. those containing words used to designate coordinated, subordinated or a higher rank within a system of meanings, as with science, philosophy, technology, etc.
d. those presenting the expression in a linguistic context or in a specific environment which, in fact, restricts the meaning or the spatial, temporal or modal sphere where it occurs; to a particular situation or to the spiritual level; to a given activity or to an occupation; to a social institution such as the government, the law, etc.
e. those providing an equivalent form for the Middle English expression in French or Latin.

This same classification has been applied in the present study under all circumstances.

3. Dates

The dates provided for each quotation containing a Scandinavian loan correspond to the date of composition and production of the manuscript, respectively, and in that order. In certain cases only one date is given, that for the composition, and that applies to the following texts: *Ayenb.*, *CT*, *TB*, *Wks.*, *Paston*, *Donet*, *Proc.Chanc.*, *RParl.*, *Barth.*

As already mentioned above, there might be a range of twenty-five years difference in the dates provided, followed by a question mark (?). In these cases followed by a question mark, the text may be later than indicated.

4. Citing texts

Besides the dates for composition and for the manuscript, I have also followed Kurath's edition of the *MED* when citing the texts themselves in the examples I have used to illustrate my analysis. In the *MED*, two types of reference are used: Titles and *incipits*. Incipits are used for short verse works that are not known by a widely accepted title, that are not included in a particular collection of medieval verse edited as a unit (i.e.: *Add.Hymnal*, Audelay *Poems*), or that are by a well-known author (Chaucer, Hoccleve). These *incipits* preserve the spelling in Brown & Robbins (1943). Abbreviated titles, on the other hand, are based, above all, on the titles provided by Wells (1916).

When a text appears in more than one version or recension, the reference includes a number in brackets (i.e.: *WBible(1)*, *WBible(2)*) or a letter (i.e.: *PPl.A*, *PPl.B*, *PPl.C*). Numbers have been also used to differentiate texts that are conventionally known with the same title, as with *Body & S. (1)* and *Body & S. (2)*.

As regards the contents of extracts or quotations, square brackets [ ] have been used for the different variants illustrating synonyms, variation in forms or in grammatical structures and spelling differences that are relevant from a phonemic point of view.

Abbreviations for titles of manuscripts as well as their complete versions are contained in the appendix to this study.

4.1. References to verse texts

Texts written in verse are quoted along with the line reference (i.e.: *Gawain* 247 or *Destr.Troy* 113). Texts divided into books, *passus*, etc., are quoted by indicating both the part and the line (i.e.: *PPl.C* 7.309; Lydg. *FP* 3.720). Other verse texts containing numbered stanzas without any alineation are cited with only the stanza number (i.e.: Jas.I *KQ* st. 52). Finally, verse texts without any indication for lines or verse numbering are cited by page number preceded by "p."

4.2. References to prose texts

The way in which prose texts are cited varies depending on how they have been edited. Texts with continuous pagination are quoted using page numbers (i.e.: *Ayenb*. 125), or by referring to page and line (i.e.: Malory *Wks*. 114/29). If a prose text has been published in several volumes with independent page numbering, both volume and page are given (i.e.: Trev. *Hidg*. 2.17).

4.3. References to the Bible

References are normally to book, chapter and verse (i.e.: *WBible* Mat.2.16; *WBible* Ps.97.5).

4.4. References for non-edited texts

Non-edited manuscripts are indicated with an asterisk. They are cited using folio, page (a= recto, b= verso) and column (a= 1st column, etc.) (i.e.: *Ancr. 28a; *Trev. Barth. 85 b/a).

5. Grammatical categories

One of the variables under analysis is that of the grammatical category of the different terms compiled. Elements which from a morphological point of view are clearly nouns, adjectives, verbs and gerunds (deverbal nouns) have separate entries, whereas participles are treated as verbs unless they occur only in adjectival constructions. Adverbs are also entered separately except for those cases in which they have no different adjectival form in later periods.

It is sometimes difficult to ascribe to a particular category those elements which are not always easy to distinguish and which Kurath calls "compounds", "combinations" and "phrases" (1956: 4). Kurath proposes separate entries for:
- asyntactic compounds, such as *up-rist*, *with-in*, etc.
- syntactic compounds which are phonetically or morphologically characterised, such as *god-fader*, *alder-first*, etc.
- compounds containing one element that has not been recorded as "simplex", or whose meaning cannot be inferred from the meanings of its constituents, as in *man-slaue*, *war-loue*, etc.
- forms derived from compounds (Kurath calls them "decompounds"), such as *ever-lastingnesse*.

There are also separate entries for compounds deriving from phrases with unaltered word order or sounds when they have a wide range of meanings or if the meaning of the whole compound can be inferred from that of its constituents.

In general, and since it is not my intention to discuss grammatical categorisation, I have accepted and adopted this classification, and the corresponding records in the database contain this type of information, following the above taxonomy.

6. Etymology

Although I will concentrate on Scandinavian loans for the purpose of this study, some prior revision of basic questions may be illuminating. I have only included those forms directly descended from a Scandinavian language (or dialect at that moment) without any interference or merger from other languages, essentially from Old English. Thus I have disregarded a few cases in which, for instance, the origin of a term is said to be Old Norse but filtered through early Middle English. In other words, I have only considered those cases in which the relation to Old Norse is absolutely direct.

Variants from the source language that, in turn, seem to be reflected in Middle English variants are given. Similarly, several alternative spellings are provided for the same form whenever they appear recorded in contemporary texts.

The meaning of the ON term is provided only when it is significantly divergent from the range of meanings of the ME word, if this is due either to an innovation produced in Middle English or to an inaccurate registry in existing dictionaries.

On some occasions, and for several different reasons, the direct source of a particular ME word is not documented. In such cases, Kurath makes reference to a similar and related word. When this is so, I have simply provided this related word as a possible source for the one in ME. In those cases in which no comment or etymological source are provided, I have decided not to include the term in my database, even though this affects the size of the corpus.

Finally, it is important to mention that the forms taken from Old Norse are not normally reconstructed in the form in which they entered English, but are normally cited in Old Icelandic or Eastern Norse forms.

7. Dialects

Another variable for our analysis is "dialect", according to which we can obtain an estimate as to the dialectal areas from which more Scandinavian loans are found, and then try to find a reason for this. The *MED* proposes a classification of texts and manuscripts according to the dialect to which they belong except, of course, quotations obtained from journals, series or books by contemporary authors. Because of this, not all terms compiled have been classified, which in turn affects frequencies. Consequently, findings here have been relativised.

Kurath's initial classification of dialects was revised and modified in the 1984 edition, the latter being more detailed. Thus, whereas Kurath's earlier edition mentions only "East Midland", the later one makes a further division into "South East Midland" and "North East Midland". In this respect, I have followed the more detailed dialectal division proposed by the 1984 editorial team, since it provides more clarity when it comes to interpreting the historical data dealt with in Chapters One and Two, as well as in the linguistic analysis.

8. Semantic fields

All the terms under survey have been classified in semantic fields using Serjeantson's proposal (1935) as a starting point. In chapter five of her classical *History of Foreign Words in English* she establishes an interesting initial list of semantic fields in which loanwords are said to appear. After a preliminary inspection of my material, however, I have added certain other fields to that list. A number is used to identify each of these semantic fields in the database, in order to speed up the introduction of data in the database and the subsequent analysis. Both the number and name of each lexico-semantic field is reproduced in Table 1.

Only "miscellaneous" here requires explanation. It could also have been labelled "others", and contains those elements that were not easily classifiable or were not easy to assign to any of the other thirty-four categories. This is the case with verbs such as PE *do*, or certain suffixes not included under 31 but which were not easily placed under "abstractions". However, for the sake of accuracy I have tried to keep the field "miscellaneous" to a minimum.

9. Spelling

Certain changes in spelling have been made to the original typography used in the *MED*. As some other editors of Old and Middle English texts have also done (Mitchell and Robinson 1997), the diacritic <:> has been used instead of a macron to indicate a particular vowel length. I have also reduced both capital "eth" and "thorn" to the grapheme <Ð>

Table 1: *Number keys assigned to semantic fields*

Key	Semantic field
1	reference to person or rank
2	reference to assemblies or groups
3	finance and trade
4	buildings, decoration, architecture
5	the law and social relations
6	religion, beliefs and rites
7	war and warfare
8	nature, geographical features
9	animal life
10	clothing, textile
11	household and other objects
12	physical action
13	eating, drinking and cookery
14	states of mind, qualities
15	mental action or action addressed to the mind
16	abstractions
17	writing, learning, painting and the arts
18	agriculture, farm life and gardening
19	medicine and anatomy, human body
20	hunting, fishing, falconry, sports and games
21	navigation and the sea
22	time
23	climate and weather
24	measuring units
25	crafts
26	sex
27	habits, history and traditions
28	miscellaneous
29	manner, mode
30	place, location
31	suffixes, in names and place-names
32	physical appearance
33	physical ability
34	movement
35	quality

Chapter Five

The lexical system of Scandinavian England

1. Introduction

In this chapter I will present the results of my analysis and I will also try to provide an interpretation for them in the light of the available historical information and also from the sociolinguistic perspective described in Chapter 3. As is customary with this type of study, graphs and figures will be used for a better understanding of findings and for a preliminary presentation of conclusions.

As mentioned above in the discussion of data selection and the corpus, I have looked at a set of variables for each of the terms that the *Middle English Dictionary* regards as being of Scandinavian origin. The study of such variables will offer valuable information about the circumstances under which borrowing (regarded as an important part of language change) occurred. In the sections that follow, each of these variables will be dealt with in some detail.

2. Dates

The year 1107 is the first date in which a Scandinavian term is recorded in early Middle English in my corpus (following *MED* dates). The entry is documented in the third volume edited by the *Early Place Name Society* dealing with the counties of Bedfordshire and Huntingdon. The entry itself is the suffix *bergh,* from Old Icelandic *berg,* used to refer to mounds or hills, and in this particular case appears in the placename *Wardeberg.* The *MED* only records one more occurrence of this suffix in the following twenty years, the term *Akeberga* appearing in 1119, in which the suffix is again part of a placename[73].

Even after 1120 the pace at which Scandinavian loans are incorporated into writing is very slow. In the following two decades I have only detected five new uses of such terms, three of them in the *Peterborough Chronicle.*

---

[73] *Early Place Name Society* 14, n. 161 devoted to Yorkshire East Riding.

The first is *bærnde*, from the verb *brennen* (ON *brenna*), from the year 1116 (estimated to have been written in 1121):

(1) On þisum ylcan geare bærnde eall þat mynstre of Burh.

In 1126, *Peterborough Chronicle* narrates the events for that same year in the following way:

(2) He sende..Hugo to Windlesofra, And let hine don on harde bande.

In this case, *bande* reflects a previous Scandinavian form (ON *band*) referring to an object similar to a shackle which was used for prisoners at the time. The final reference recorded in the *Peterborough Chronicle* for this twenty-year period dates from 1131. Once again it is a form of the verb *brennen*:

(3) On an Mone niht...wæs se heouene o ðe norð half eall swilc hit wære bærnenede fir.

Table 2 sets out the raw frequencies of terms recorded between 1100 and 1200 in subperiods of twenty years. Although it is often claimed that language change can usefully be observed in lapses of thirty years (Kytö, Smitterrberg and Rudanko 2000), I have resorted to smaller periods here for a more detailed account of the pace at which borrowing was operating in these first years of the Middle English period:

Table 2. *Raw frequencies for borrowing in eME.*

Years	Loanwords
1100-1120	2
1121-1140	5
1141-1160	23
1161-1180	18
1181-1200	213

The increase of Scandinavian origin terms detected from 1180 onwards deserves some attention. One of the first things to be considered is the Norman Conquest of 1066. When Duke William of Normandy arrived in England its population was basically Anglo-Saxon and Scandinavian since, as we saw in the first chapter, native Celtic tribes had been pushed to the west of Watling Street from the fifth century onwards by different waves of Germanic newcomers. Both communities, Anglo-Saxons and Scandinavians, shared a common Germanic descent and had been coexisting for around a century when the Norman troops came over from the Continent. There is no way we can know the degree of acquaintance between the Anglo-Saxon and Scandinavian communities at the time (their social networks density in Milroyan terms) but they may well have not been homogeneous.

Using the communities in the Danelaw as a reference, we can suppose that they were not in general very large settlements (except, perhaps, for York and the other cities in the Territory of the Five Boroughs) in which the two ethnic groups seem to be have intermingled. At this point in time, neighbours may have identified themselves and one another as descending from one or the other group, as is to be observed in present-day rural societies when the members of families are often given nicknames referring to their geographical origin. Such communities would probably be multiplex (multiple relations) and considerably dense. This again would lead us to infer that the linguistic situation was one in which most speakers knew their mother tongue's colloquial variety as well as that of the foreign language, a situation which Iglesias Rábade (1992) calls primary or natural semibilingualism.

It is important to bear in mind again that we are referring to a largely illiterate population and to a situation in which the relation between writing and speech was extremely slow, in the sense that from the moment that a particular linguistic habit began being spread to the moment when it was finally recorded in writing (if ever, see Bator 2009), a considerable period of time may have elapsed[74].

To these two factors we must add the type of speech community receiving the invaders, and also its cultural level, another determining social circumstance. Although a certain degree of segregation in the different settlements with mixed population (native and Scandinavian) may have existed, it is very likely that they united to fight a common enemy coming from the outside, especially, as was the case of the Norman Conquest, the menace was very real and disrupted the prevailing social order.

The linguistic consequences of this third factor can be immediately deduced: a greater cohesion among the members of a community implies a

---

74   The dominance of orality over writing at the time was such that we may never get to know the real number of Scandinavian terms that were actually used, since many of them may have disappeared without ever being written down. Such terms were perhaps the result of some temporary fashion or simply they denoted things that were not considered appropriate for writing.

higher degree of communication and this inevitably implies more interaction between the two language groups. Thus, from ca. 1180 the frequency with which Scandinavian terms are detected increases notably in my data, by a factor of one hundred. The type of terms introduced in English also seem to be more diverse. From an initial situation in which almost all loanwords referred to place-names, we turn to one in which personal names and substantives abound. Example (4) below is illustrative:

(4) Normannus le Bonde (*Pipe Roll Society*, 29, n. 103)

This name is recorded in a legal document and behaves exactly as described above, with *Normannus* (PE *Norman*) identifying someone through his geographical origin ("man from the North") at the same time as *le Bonde* makes reference to his social condition (from ON *bonda*). At this point nouns referring to different occupations also begin to appear. Such is the case with *bu(:)te-carl* (PE *boatman*) or *clubber, clobber* (someone who makes clubs). The following examples, (5) and (6) have the same identificative aim as (4).

(5) Wuluardus Butekarl (Feet of Fines in the Public Record Office of the Tenth year of King Richard I in Pipe Roll Society, 24, n. 34)

(6) Turstanus Clober (Palgrave 1835: 414)

In (6) we can observe that both elements in the name are of Scandinavian origin, *Turstanus* being the latinised version of ON *Ðórsteinn*. At the beginning of the thirteenth century, once the Norman power is well established in England, the number of Scandinavian loans recorded decreases, although they are now more varied. Verbs such as ME *adlen* (still to be found nowadays in the Yorkshire area meaning "to earn"[75]), *angren* ("to provoke or offend someone"), *atlen* ("to plan" also used with the meaning of "to advance"), and certain forms of ON *va(:)ron* will become part of the paradigm of OE *beon/wesan*, as is the case with *ware* in:

(7) Ðu art nu to daiȝ alswa ðu ware ðas daiȝes (*Vices and Virtues* 145/23).

Graph 1 represents the dates in which Scandinavian loanwords under examination entered English. The x-axis represents periods of twenty years. The

---

75 The expression *to adle one's brass* meaning to earn one's living is still in use in Yorkshire.

period between numbers 1 and 2, then, corresponds to 1100 to 1120, with the period 1540 to 1550 the last one recorded here.

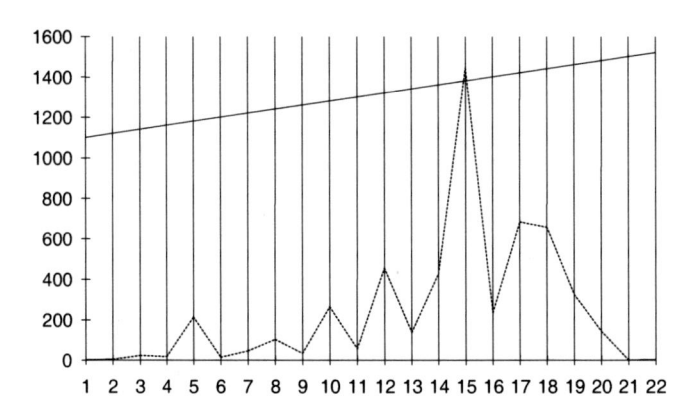

Graph 1.   Scandinavian Loanwords entering English (1100-1550)

As Graph 1 shows 1381-1400 is the period for which most occurrences of Scandinavian loans have been found (1,444 tokens). At the time, the English language seems to have assimilated most neologisms arriving from Northern Europe as well as those coming from France. Such assimilation is evident in writing. This is what happens in many of the texts composed by Chaucer (Smith and Samuels 1988). For instance, almost all entries for the *Canterbury Tales* are dated (according to the *MED*) around 1385. All sorts of terms with a North Germanic origin can be found here. Thus we again find ME *brennynge*, from ON *brenna*. This particular verb form also exhibits the ending -*ing* which characterises a Northern present participle as opposed to the traditional OE endings -*ande*, -*ende*:

(8) The grete clamour..That the ladyes made at the brennynge Of the bodies ("The Knight's Tale", A.996).

We can also find new verbs such as *callen* (ON *kalla*) in *Troylus and Cryseyde* around the same period as illustrated in example (9):

(9) He gan awake, And gan to calle (*Troylus and Cryseyde*, 2.71)

Certain nouns that have acquired a widespread use to refer to a very specific social condition, as is the case of *bonde*, used in example (10) below as the antonym of *free* appear:

(10) Fortune..pleyeth with free and bonde (*Troylus and Cryseyde* 1.84)

Another text showing a high number of Scandinavian forms in this twenty-year period is the *Wyclifite Bible*. The *Middle English Dictionary* makes a difference between the early (1) and late (2) versions, the early one coinciding with this period, and late version not appearing until the beginning of the fifteenth century. The *MED* often provides alternative terms appearing in the later version, as we can see in the case of *bleckid* and *maad blak* in the following example:

(11) My skin is bleckid [WB(2): maad blak; L denigrata] vp on me, and my bones drieden for hete (*Wyclifite Bible* (1), Job 30.30)

The frequency of loans recorded in my corpus decreases from the beginning of the fifteenth century onwards. This is not due to the fact that the terms have ceased to be used in all social contexts, but rather to the fact that more prolific authors, such as Chaucer, have by now stopped writing. It is easier to find more Scandinavian terms used in these authors simply because they wrote a more extensive body of work. The decrease is also caused by the fact that certain works, such as the early version of the *Wyclifite Bible,* whose pages contain many originally Old Norse terms, had by now been completed.

All in all, the increased use of Scandinavian terms in the last twenty years of the thirteenth century can be considered highly significant, since it can be clearly be accounted for by language contact.

3. Dialects

As already mentioned, the study of the data relating to dialectal areas was considered important for the study not only of Scandinavian loans in English but also for the account of how these loans spread throughout the territory as reflected in different ME geographical varieties. Middle English dialectology is a widely studied field, with a tradition dating back to the nineteenth century (Skeat 1911) and finding its most exciting point in the twentieth century with the application of modern sociolinguistic techniques to ancient texts in *A Linguistic Atlas of Late Medieval English* (McIntosh et al 1987). Indeed, dialectology has always been taken to constitute one of the branches of (historical) linguistics, and has provided excellent overviews of the English language throughout this period.

According to the most widely accepted hypothesis, the dialects corresponding to the Danelaw are those with a higher influence of Scandinavian languages and in which we can, consequently, find a higher number of loans from these languages. In principle, such dialects correspond to the areas Northern, North-East Midlands and East Midlands, according to Robert E. Lewis's classification for the *MED*. However, it can be seen in Graph 2 that our data do not coincide with this assumption. The horizontal axis shows the different dialects that I have taken into consideration, as well as another element labelled "standard" (in many cases called "common core"). As explained in the description of the selection and compilation of the corpus in Chapter 4, terms have been assigned to different dialects according to the criteria proposed by Lewis (1984) in his description of the texts. As Kurath (1956: 10) had noted when editing the *MED*, only forms "containing striking dialect features either as relics or as innovations" are ascribed to particular dialects, including the literary dialect of the London area. This statement leads me to believe that all texts that have not been classified as belonging to a distinctive dialectal variety should belong to the so-called "standard".

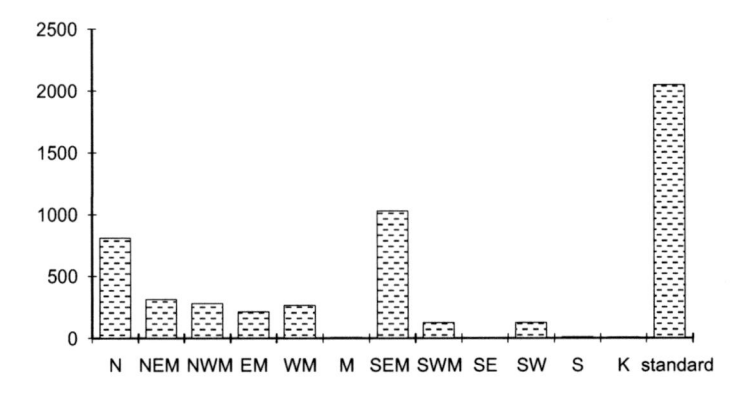

Graph 2.   Dialectal distribution of Scandinavian loans in English.

The vertical axis of Graph 2 contains the number of Scandinavian terms for each of the dialects and for the standard on a scale from 0 to 2500, these counts being of raw frequencies. Clearly, a cursory glance tells us that it is not in the Danelaw dialects that neologisms can be found most abundantly. On the contrary, it is the so-called "common core" vocabulary that contains a higher proportion of such terms, the 2048 tokens from this "common core" representing 38.67% of the corpus, a very high percentage indeed. If we focus on the dialects containing fewest uses of Scandinavian terms, we see that it is the South (S) and South-East (SE) dialects. I have in fact found only four uses of Scandinavian origin terms for the S and nine for the SE varieties. Certainly, the terms appearing in texts from the South-Eastern area are often of common, widespread use even nowadays. Thus, we find *anger* ("suffering, problem"), *bond* ("mutual obligation acquired through marriage"), *brinie* ("coat of mail") and the verb *brennen* ("burn, torture by fire") in the following cases:

(12) Owte ofe worldly noyse and of worldly angyrse and besynes (Perry 1867; 53/18)

(13) Many walde be in religyon, bot þay may noghte..for band of Maryage (Perry 1867: 51/3)

(14) Helm and brenie (Morris 1867-1868)

(15) ȝe seneȝden alse lange alse ȝe lefede and ȝe scule birne alse longe as ic lefie (Morris 1867-1868)

As for the loans found in texts from the South, it must be said that with the exception of one, all are from a single collection of legends extracted from different manuscripts. In this case, all Scandinavian words occur in the same text, *The Southern Passion* (Brown 1927), none before the end of the thirteenth century:

(16) Wher ich am, my seruant wiþ me ale-gate is (*The Southern Passion*, (Pep) 196)

In (16), the adverb *ale-gate* is based on an Old Norse phrase recorded in the Icelandic literary register as *alla-gotu* and that has given place to its PE *always*[76] equivalent.

Example (17) contains OI *kasta*, ME *cast*, which on this occasion means "to toss a coin":

(17) Ak caste we lot, who shal hit haue (*The Southern Passion*, (Pep) 1500).

---

[76] Let us bear in mind that ON *gotu*, from which we obtain ME *gate*, means "way, path".

The only example that is not found in this collection of legends is contained in *The Assumption of Our Lady*:

(18) Thow woldest not be-leue, Thomas..euer thu leuys amysse in minde (Lumby & McKnight 1866).

In this quotation (from 1485) we can observe the use of *amysse*, an adverb that corresponds to the Old Icelandic *a(:)mis*.

Most of these terms occurring in the South and South-East dialectal areas are now very common in English. However, we should not consider their small number (thirteen occurrences in my corpus) to be evidence of the scarce penetration of Scandinavian linguistic habits, but as evidence of exactly the opposite.

The historical events described at the beginning of this study remind us that there existed from the year 793 a constant demographic pressure, exerted mainly by the Danes from the Eastern and Northern coasts towards inland territory, as they searched for new settlements. This would seem to imply that the South and South-East areas were precisely those with a lower number of continental inhabitants. But this area is also where London, Oxford and Cambridge are to be found, forming a geographical triangle that would be of paramount importance in the development of the English language. The area around these cities, indeed, is responsible for producing a great many works of all kinds, since the Universities in Oxford and Cambridge are not only centres of prestige but are also highly productive in terms of texts. Indeed, certain literary styles and cultural trends appear here first, and local linguistic habits also tend spread to the rest of the country, especially from the 13th century onwards, once Norman rule has been firmly established. The court also tends to use this particular variety, which will become the standard (although there has been some recent discussion about the true origins of the standard, see Fisher 1996, Wright 2000, Montoya and Moskowich 2003). In other words, this variety constitutes what I have been calling the "common core".

According to my findings, and given that no other study has explored this possibility, it could be argued that so few tokens of Scandinavian terms are found in those dialects considered relevant from a cultural and social point of view due to the fact that Kurath (1956) decided to record them as dialectally unmarked, since they were not very peculiar or unusual in nature. This implies that many other originally Scandinavian items were being used in the

Middle Ages in this part of England, but that they were not regarded as a differentiating dialectal feature or as marked in any other manner since they were in widespread use[77].

This same reason would explain why more Scandinavian terms are found in what I have labelled as STANDARD in Graph 2 than in the dialect corresponding to the Danelaw (SEM). The corpus contains 1027 uses of Scandinavian words in the SEM dialect, and this is the dialect with the greatest number of tokens. Table 3 below, on the contrary, illustrates the number of types collected for each dialect, ordered from the highest (Standard) to the lowest (South-East).

Table 3. Scandinavian loans and dialectal areas.

Dialect	Scandinavian tokens
STANDARD	2048
SEM	1027
N	809
NEM	313
NWM	281
WM	264
EM	213
SWM	125
K	46
S	9
M	7
SE	4

Examples abound, and only those containing the terms appearing most often have been reproduced here. The phrase *haven ado(:)* from ON infinitive *at do(:)* is often used as a noun. In example (19) it makes reference to sexual

---

[77] According to López Morales (1989: 55) "La diferencia entre un cambio en marcha y otro ya muy avanzado puede notarse en su distribución social. El cambio comienza en un grupo de cualquier punto de la escala; cuando se desarrolla y se expande a otros grupos, todavía puede verse el patrón piramidal a través del parámetro generacional, con los niveles más altos entre los jóvenes del grupo original. Cuando el cambio se generaliza, con frecuencia se estigmatiza la forma perdedora" and with the data gathered it could be inferred that language change, as regards Scandinavian loans, has advanced to such an extent in the period under study that most forms are not stigmatised at all but standardised.

intercourse, but it may also have meanings such as "conflict", "commercial relation", "traffic" or "difficulty".

(19) Thiestes was presumptuous..With Europa my wiff to haue a-do (Bergen 1924: 121-3)

And, of course, it is also found as the verb *to do*:

(20) My fader and I must..shewe unto hym our gode assystens..in such maters as he shall have a doo (Gairdner 1904: 5.19)

Another term whose use is widely extended in the SEM dialect and in the standard is ME *ai* and its different spelling variants (*aʒʒ, ay(e), ei*). The origin of this time adverb is ON *ai*, OI *ei* and it means "always", "all the time" as illustrated in examples (21) and (22):

(21) þi man y wil be & serue þe ay þer while mi liif lest may (Zupitza 1883; 49, 59)

(22) His libertee this brid desireth ay (Manly & E. Rickert 1940: H. 174).

ME *al-gate* (cf. supra) is another frequently occurring term and it is not only restricted to this dialect. An adverb, it is constantly used by authors such as Gower, Chaucer, Capgrave, etc., since from the first half of the fourteenth century it is part of the vocabulary of most speakers of English.

(23) Bot his harp he tok algate, And dede him barfot out atte ʒate (*Orfeo*, 231, in Sisam 1925)

To conclude this review of Chaucer's dialect, I will offer another example of a term in common use. The adverb *aloft(e)*, from ON, OI *a(:) lopti* is used to refer to a place that is higher (also in a figurative sense). Thus, in the romance of *Merlin* it denotes a physical space:

(24) Thei..brought hym vp to a windowe a-lofte (Wheatley 1865)

However, there are examples in which ME *alofte* refers to the position someone occupies on the social ladder, as used by John Gower:

(25) He that stant to day alofte..Tomorwe he falleth (*Confessio Amantis*, 4.2216, in Macaulay 1900)

Considering that the Midlands was an area heavily inhabited by Danes, it is reasonable to ask why only seven tokens belonging to this dialect are found in all the material. The reason may lie in the fact that most texts have already been ascribed to "partial" areas within the Midlands (East, West, North or South) and only a few, due to their difficult localisation, have been left as "Midlands", with no further detail.

The rest of the dialectal varieties where other terms found can be included do not show significant differences as regards the number of tokens they have. In fact, all contain around two hundred elements and most of these are also used in texts I have classified as not belonging to any particular dialect but to the common unmarked variety rather.

Only Northern English seems to exhibit forms that have penetrated other areas and which are, therefore, clearly identifiable as diatopic features. In this way, *ein-domi* (equivalent to "the right to act for oneself"), obtained directly from its original Old Icelandic form, is found in ME *aindain* or *aidom*. The meaning of the English version of this adjective is not very clear, although it seems to be something like "Sovereign; singular" as in example (26):

(26) Quat, & has þou ossed to Alexander þis ayndain (Skeat 1886)

The evidence, then, points towards a preeminent use of Scandinavian terms in the "common core". Although other authors have not provided information concerning this, my findings seems to show that such uses are deeply rooted and are not specific to or characteristic of particular geographical or social areas; had this not been the case, they would have never been integrated into the standard.

4. Semantic fields

It seemed relevant to this particular study of language change to consider semantic fields as a variable, not least to help verify (or not) the claim that Scandinavian terms in English belong to the colloquial or everyday life register and are, to a certain extent, restricted to these.

The thirty-five semantic fields mentioned above in Chapter 4, Section 8 have been used to classify all the terms in the analysis. The resulting counts are offered in Table 4 below, where only the numeric keys assigned to each of those fields (see Chapter 4 on "Plan and method"). It should be noted that the column on the right refers to each of the uses of a term, that is to say, to the particular meaning a term acquires in a particular context, in order to avoid the natural interferences that polysemy otherwise might have caused:

Table 4.   Scandinavian loanwords per semantic field

FIELD	TOKENS
1	208
2	25
3	42
4	89
5	333
6	73
7	80
8	160
9	111
10	121
11	189
12	859
13	62
14	422
15	360
16	296
17	64
18	117
19	230
20	94
21	110
22	105
23	12
24	40
25	59
26	8
27	7
28	121
29	213
30	100
31	194
32	166
33	5
34	156
35	64

Differences between semantic fields are clear. Graph 3 offers this same information in a more direct, visual presentation.

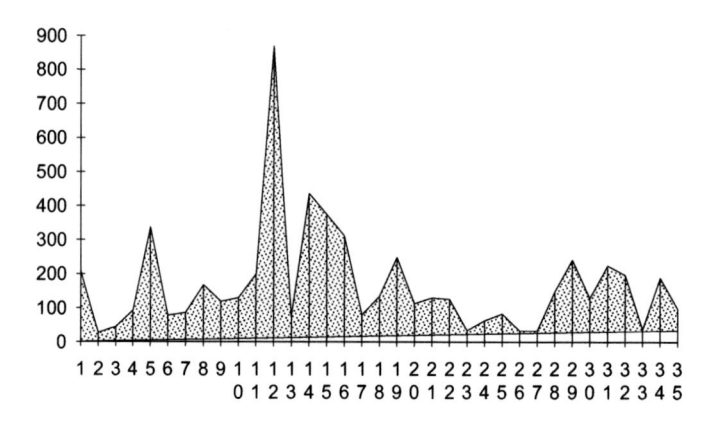

Graph 3. Distribution of Scandinavian loans in semantic fields

As can be observed the lexical field with the highest number of Scandinavian neologisms is the one containing the terms relating to physical actions (12), accounting for 16.2 % of all 5,295 uses found. Some of these terms are part of phrases or idiomatic expressions and, curiously enough, they are frequently from the most commonly used terms in the language, those mentioned above as part of the standard or unmarked variety. Such is the case of the ME adverb *aloft(e)*, appearing in several phrases such as *holden alofte* whose meaning is "to continue or go on with something" as in the following example:

(27) Ðe olde lorde of þat leude Couþe wel halde layk alofte (Gollancz 1940)

ME *maken alofte* means "begin, start" the same as ME *raisen alofte* in the two examples here:

(28) He made his paly aloft, His gammes he gan kiþe (McNeill 1940)

(29) Whi þat werre was reised olofte (Hearne 1725)

Other terms indicating physical action are represented not by phrases or set expressions, but by Scandinavian verbs. In fact, this is the most abundant category within this semantic field, with 721 out of 859 terms (83.9%) relating to physical action used as verbs. Among them we can consider some illustrative examples:

(30) Ðan etils him sir Alexander (Skeat 1886)

(31) Jason..gripes his weppon, Armur & all thing atlet before (Panton and Donaldson 1869)

In (30) and (31), *etils* and *atlet* are forms of the verb ME *atlen* ("prepare" or "get ready") that can be also found as *aghtel, haghtil, attel, etlen* and *aghtil*. In all of these forms the original ON **ahtil-* can be easily recognised.

Verbs referring to "show" as ME *aunen* appear in early texts, such as the *Ormulum*:

(32) Herode king Wass gramm..son summ himm awwnedd wass off þatt kalldisskenn genge (Ker 1940)

as do verbs referring even to such specific actions as to put money inside one's own bag:

(33) He..bagged hem [gold nobles] and coffred at the last (Furnivall 1886)

Of course, many of the actions described are related to the human body, as is the case with ME *be(:)len*, "swell, inflame" from ON *bæ(:)la* (whose original meaning was "to burn, to sting").

(34) His kne..was so bremly bolned and belyd, þat he myght noȝt wele it weld (Fowler 1891)

ME *brennen* seems to be the most abundant verb in this group. I have chosen some fragments to illustrate how *-ing* forms are used, as opposed to the corresponding native ones with *-ande, -ende,* when referring to concepts. According to the *MED* classification of grammatical categories, these *-ing* forms are gerunds and they appear only infrequently as present participles. Nevertheless, this is still evidence that interference also occurred at a grammatical level (Czerniak 2011). In example (35), *brenning* (from ON *brenna*) means "destruction by fire":

(35) Landis to wynne, and nat wyth slaght and wyth brennynge (Furnivall 1896)

Some of these verbs are still part of present-day English common core vocabulary, as they were in the past. Thus, we preserve ON *kalla* in PE *to call*, a verb that came down to us through ME *callen* (sometimes found with the more clearly Scandinavian spelling *kallen*):

(36) He..calde oft, 'Bermen, bermen, hider swiþe!' (Skeat 1868)

The use of this verb was so deeply rooted that certain authors whose language variety is considered to be distant from Scandinavian influence, such as Chaucer, cannot but include it in their texts:

(37) He..called evere in his compleynte Her name (*Troylus and Cryseyde* in Robinson (ed.) 1957)

The same phenomenon occurs with the verb ME *casten*, which has many different acceptions during the Middle Ages. There are numerous examples in my corpus, but in the one below it means "To throw (sth.) to a distance, fling, hurl":

(38) Go forth thy wey, or I wol caste a stoon (The Miller's Prologue and Tale, A.3712, in Manlyand Rickeit (eds.) 1940)

The next lexical field according to number of loans is that concerning state of mind (number key 14), containing 422 tokens of Scandinavian loans in all, and arguably refers to a realm of everyday life, given that different states of mind and moods are part of human nature. It seems that the number of tokens found contradicts the popular idea that the Danes and Norwegians were people interested only in raiding and plundering, an assumption which made earlier scholars believe that Scandinavian words in English were limited to the spheres of survival and material wealth. On the contrary, the terms found in my data (7.9 % of all) do not seem to suggest this, but rather a human nature exposed to spiritual experiences too. Example (39) contains the verb ME *adlen* from OI *oðla-sk* with the meaning of "to deserve glory, spiritual peace" (some of this verb's meanings would belong to other semantic fields, as explained above):

(39) Niss nan oþerr kinness lif Ðat addleþþ eche blisse (Ker 1940)

In this same sense of mental or emotional state, there are certain uses whose meanings are ambiguous, as in the case of (40) below, where the adjective ME *alod, olod* (probably originating from a plural participle OI *af-lo(:)a*) makes reference to something "in a bad condition":

(40) Therfor I drede lest god on vs will take veniance, ffor syn is now alod without any repentance (England and Pollard 1897)

Another adjective taken from the Scandinavian languages comes from the OI noun *ang-r*, whose meaning is "sorrow, trouble" and which appears in ME as *ange*, very often in impersonal constructions:

(41) Himm wass waȝȝ & ange Off þatt he nohht ne wisste off Crist (Ker 1940)

The fact that the newcomers had some kind of mental and spiritual depth (too often denied by describing them as greedy, violent and bellicose) can be attested in the traces they left in the English language. The third most abundant semantic field is, indeed, the one referring to mental actions, identified as number 5 in my database. The number of neologisms is also high here (360 tokens), and once again many of them are parts of phrases, together with certain verb forms such as *holden up herte alofte* ("preserve (one's) courage or strength"):

(42) Forwhi good hope halt up hire herte o-lofte (*Troylus and Cryseyde* 5.348, in Robinson 1957)

leden amis ("to cheat")

(43) They seken good, but þey ben led amys Be errour of th[eir]e owne wrecchidness (Schtimmer 1914: 263)

speken amis o *saien amis* ("to tell lie", *amis* is sometimes used with the sense of "wrongly")

(44) Haue me excused if I speke amys; My wyl is good (*The Squire's Prologue, Tale, Squire-Franklin Link, including the Words of the Host to the Franklin*, F.7, Manly and Rickert, (eds.) (1940),)

(45) Yf y amys seye, amende me (Zupitza 1875)

reden amis ("to advice wrongly")

(46) Ðei red him alle a mysse, þat conseil gaf þerto (Hearne 1725: 164)

don amis ("to offend", "to do something bad or to do wrong on purpose"), and many others.

(47) ȝif a man haþ don amis And foule sinneþ haþ iwrouht (Morrill 1898)

Although my examples include many terms that are not part of phrases, the examples provided above may be enough by way of illustration.

Laws and social relations are also well represented, with a total of 333 tokens (6.3% of the corpus). This may give us an idea about the speakers originally using these terms, and it again reinforces the hypothesis that the Scandinavian settlers of England were not the wild tribes traditionally portrayed in English historical records. They are, rather, speakers whose lexicon either fills specific gaps in OE (concepts which may not have existed previously in Anglo-Saxon society) or refer to something which assumes so great a significance for those Scandinavian speakers that the terms brought from the continent are superimposed onto already existing ones in the recipient languages[78]. Some instances are included in phrases as illustrated below:

(48) Wicked iuges..tume amys doomes by-cause of couetyse (Holmstedt 1933: 236/15)

In (48) the ME phrase *turnen amis* means "to pervert justice". In (49), however, we do not have a phrase[79] but a verb which is frequently used, since it has different meanings. ME *atlen* from ON **ahtil*- means "to name someone as heir":

(49) She was eldist & heire etlit to his londes (Panton and Donaldson 1869: 394)

Another example clearly belonging to the legal sphere is ME *lesen benk* (with alternative spellings *ben(g)ke*, *bink*) whose second element originates in OI *bekkr*, comparable to the Danish and Swedish forms *bänk*. The meaning of the whole is "to lose one's position as a judge" as can be inferred in the following extract from a text by Mannyng:

(50) Ðe first justise in benk, Sir Thomas of Weland, For falshed & for wrenk he forsuore þe land..He departed with gram, & þe benk les (Hearne 1725: 246)

The ME phrase *crien benk* also belongs to the same semantic field and is formed by the same Scandinavian noun (*bekkr*) whose meaning is "to gather a court of law". In fact, ME *benk* may refer both to the object it designates (the

---

[78] It must be borne in mind that there have been very well-known cases, such as the one of ON *taka* and OE *niman*, where the surviving term is the Scandinavian one (see Rynell 1948; Moskowich, 2005).

[79] I use the term "phrase" here as it is used in the *MED*. The type of unit it refers to has been labelled differently depending on the theoretical framework adopted.

actual bench where judges sit while everyone else stands) and to the group of judges forming the court of law:

(51) If alle þe men now vnder mone To deme vs were brouʒt on benke (Linow 1889: 95)

The legal term of Scandinavian origin which makes itself most evident in this study is ON *logu*, "law". It is not included in my data since it falls outside the scope of this corpus and has not been sampled, which has a clear influence in the final counts for this lexical field. That is, had I taken "law" into account the word counts for this particular field would have been different and certainly higher (see Chapter 4 above). However, certain compounds in which the element appears have been found. In this way, the ME noun *bi(:)-laue* and its variants *bilage, beolaw* are integrated by two elements, both Scandinavian: ON *by*, denoting a certain type of settlement (Cameron 1977, 1978, 1990) and ON *logu*. They refer to a set of regulations for the organisation of daily life in villages, religious houses, etc. It must have been used to denote a new concept for social organisation in Anglo-Saxon England, something that did not exist before, in that it appears in Latin texts such as the extract from the regulations of Augustine monks in Canterbury:

(52) Si contingat quaestionem moveri inter nos & archiepiscopum vel ejus tenentes de substractionibus, purpresturis, dampnis seu allis injuriis hinc inde factis, quod consuetudo illa quae dicitur Bilage observetur.[80]

For the same reason, we can find this same term in texts (mostly in records) that reflect the linguistic effects of the Norman Conquest. In fact, the fragment below is not written in English yet still contains the word *Bilaews*:

(53) Inhabitants dun ville sauns ascun custome poient fayre ordinaunces ou Bilawes pur reparation del Eglise.[81]

The concepts we could label as "abstractions" constitute another well represented semantic field (number 6). On the same lines as what has so far been discussed, I have found lexical evidence that Danes and Swedes were able to introduce into the English linguistic system not only terms denoting objects or daily life events, but also abstract terms. The only sensible way to account

---

80 W. Thorn, *Chronica*, Angl. Script. (1652: 1936).
81 *Yearbook 44 of the reign of Edward III*, Selden Society 19.

for this phenomenon is to accept very close relations between the speakers of both languages. Some examples from 296 tokens gathered for this semantic group are given in (54)-(57):

(54) Lord, gyf me þir angers all. I wroght þe werk..Wharfore we haue þis dole lik dele (Heuser and Foster 1930)

Anger is the Scandinavian term in this extract, from OI *angr*, although it may also have been influenced by L *angor*. In this particular example it has the sense of "trouble, affliction". Another loan, one which is still alive in English today and which can be traced from the early thirteenth century, is ME *aue*, (alternative spellings are *au(w)e*, *aʒ (h)e*, *awaʒe*, *ahe*). In Icelandic literary texts it appears as *agi*, from ON **aga*. However, in the following quotation, it does not mean "awe" but "danger, terror" since semantic change has occurred:

(55) Leunes and beres him wile to-dragen, And fleges sen on him non agen (Morris, 865: 192)

I have shown on numerous occasions that a particular term does not belong to one lexical field or another, but that its users associate the term with different fields depending on the context. When revising certain medieval texts I have found Scandinavian loans whose immediate referent is some kind of material object but, since they were used in a figurative sense, they must be considered as belonging to the field of abstractions. This is the case with ME *bark, berk*, from OI *bork-r*. This noun usually refers to the bark of trees or bushes. Notwithstanding, in the following fragment it is metaphorically used as "superficial or outer part":

(56) Alle þe reuelaciouns..haue goostly bemenynges..& þerfore late us pike of þe rouʒ bark, & fede us of þe swete kyrnel (Hodgson 1944: 107/16)

The forms of the verb *to be* are perhaps the most relevant contributions of North Germanic dialects to English. Among them, ME *wa(:)ren* (past participle of ME *be(:)n*) directly originated in ON **va(:)ron*[82]. On a more abstract level it means "to occur, to happen, to have the necessity". It frequently appears in impersonal constructions:

---

82 It must be noted, as the *MED* points out, that Middle English preserves the same vowel.

(57) Me wore leuere i wore lame (Skeat 1868 : 1938)

In my analysis of semantic fields, medical terms as well as those relating to human anatomy come next. Such terms appear 230 times (4.3 %), and among them is ME *ancle, ankel* (from ON *ok(k)la*), which deserves some attention since it has remained in English until today as PE *ankle*. Of course, these loans do not always appear in technical texts[83], although the field would seem to be quite a learned one. In what follows I present only two examples, the first from a text which could be classified as technical, the second from the romance *Arthour and Merlin*:

(58) Let þe seke holde boþe his fete in þe watir till þe ankles (Gösta Frisk 1949)

(59) In blod he stode..in to þe anclowe (Kölbing 1890)

The use of this type of term can be observed in texts such as those by Guy de Chauliac. They are often scientific texts offering explanations of one sort or another, such as the one below in (60) about cancer, in which the loan obtained from OI *angra* is adapted to ME *angring(e)* "irritation":

(60) Of vicerez & wondez is caused a Cancre, when þat for angryng or prouoking wiþ sharp þinges.[84]

Among the clichés about the Scandinavian settlers of England is the one about their very democratic way of life and their peculiar, apparently not very hierarchical, social organisation. This question is a matter of anthropology and history, not linguistics. Notwithstanding, there are certain aspects of the settlers' society that must be taken into account in a sociolinguistic study like the present one. For this reason, I have looked at some examples in terms of how they describe the field or rank of a person. I found 208 examples, compared to only 25 examples of reference to an assembly or group. This might lead us to hypothesise that:

1) Scandinavian society was not as democratic and assembly-based as it might at first seem. There is no evidence of the sense of solidarity that has

---

83 Vid. Iglesias Rábade and Moskowich (1997).
84 *Anonymous Translation of Guy de Chauliac's Grande Chirurgie*, 87 a/b, Microfilm Print of New York Academy of Medicine MS.

been often described, in which all members of a community were a mere group of Viking sailors.

2) Many of the terms within this sphere may have belonged to the Common Germanic trunk, long before Old English split from it and acquired its own specific characteristics. It is possible that such terms had already been integrated in the language before the two languages came into contact in England.

Be this as it may, some illustrative examples are shown in (61) and (62), where the noun *amboht*, "female serf" reflects its equivalent ON *amba(:)tt*.:

(61) Icc amm ammbohht all bun To follʒhenn Godess wille (Ker 1940: 783 1. 2329)

Perhaps, the most widely known term in the semantic field denoting assemblies or groups of people is ME *by* used nowadays in place-names to designate the original site of a farm or small village:

(62) Balder bern was non in bi (Zupitza 1883: 384)

In order of frequency of use of Scandinavian loans, just above the field including terms for everyday life and household objects (number 11) we can find the one containing suffixes and placenames (number 31). The field for household, however, is placed ninth in order of frequency rates. This may indicate that it is not as important as it has often been claimed, often with no real quantitative linguistic data.

The following fields are lower down the frequency of use scale. Thus, the field of nature (number 8) has 50 tokens, as in the following example dating from ca. 1200:

(63) Downe I ley me vpon this *banke* Vnder this bryght sterre (Block, (1922)

Animal life (number 9) is represented by 11 tokens, as in the two following examples:

(64) Wormes shall in you brede as bees dos in the *byke* (England and Pollard 1897)

(65) Ðe knyʒt kachez his caple (Gollancz 1940: 2175)

and the category clothes and textiles (number 10) contains 121 occurrences.

In the following example we can observe the penetration of OI *baggi*, still in use in PE *bag*:

(66) Grete bagges ful of golde and syluer (Clubb 1953: 3.4.50 b)

A little more numerous (189 tokens) is the field containing terms designating household and other daily-life objects (number 11). We could say that this field together with 8, 9 and 10 are somehow related, all making reference to daily life in medieval England. In the same vein, field 18 might also be said to be related, its 118 tokens representing references to agriculture, vegetation and farm-life:

(67) An almtre: alnus..vinus, vimus (Herrtage 1881)

(68) Nazarzæþ bitacneþþ..brodd & blome (Ker 1940 l.10773)

Among the semantic fields relating to the physical sphere, we might mention the one I have called "appearance" (number 32), which contains 166 tokens.

The apparently low proportion of terms relating to the sea (110 uses), especially when we consider the excellent reputation the Scandinavians had as sailors, is very significant in that it is a very specific and restricted field compared, for instance, to the 859 tokens found in the far more general field of "physical action". One of the nautical terms entering Middle English from Old Norse is *bowgh* as attested by Sandahl (1951) in his classic work *Middle English Sea Terms*:

(69) Chaynes in the Bowgh of the seide Bote..Chaynes of yron in the Bowes of the seid Bote ij (Sandahl 1951: 1, 3)

Semantic field number 3, whose extra-linguistic referent is finance and trade, is found in a lower number of Scandinavian loans. I have recorded only 42 uses, which is very strange if we take into consideration the fact that commercial intercourse existed between the two peoples (Moskowich and Crespo 2007). One possible explanation for the scarcity of these loans in my corpus is the fact that commercial relations between the Isles and the North of Europe had been established long before, as research on pre-Viking times reveals (Hines 1984), so that little new vocabulary was needed in this already settled realm of activity.

Other terms with scant presence in the corpus are those designating architectural elements (number 4) with 89 tokens, religion and rites (number 6) with 73 tokens, and culture, learning, painting, writing and other related topics (number 17) with 64 tokens. It seems clear that this can be explained by the fact that the related vocabulary here was adopted by the Scandinavians from the Anglo-Saxon substratum.

Neologisms referring to sports and games (number 20) and crafts and occupations (number 25) are slightly more numerous, perhaps because certain new activities were imported into England by the newcomers, together with the words referring to them.

Lastly, as regards the field I have labelled "miscellaneous" (number 28), I have placed few terms here since most loans were easily classified within other fields.

The evidence from the corpus, then, leads us to discard the theory that most terms of Scandinavian origin in Middle English are the ones traditionally called "everyday life terms". On the contrary, there is a wide variety of semantic fields in which such terms abound. I believe that what often happened in past research was that there was a confusion between the words of everyday life with those rooted in the "common core" vocabulary of the English language.

Table 5. Loans per text-type

Text-type	Tokens
Didactic texts	1607
Romances	880
Records and minutes	730
Poetry	402
Fiction	398
Technical texts	248
Mixed texts	216
Medical	206
Vocabularies	192
Drama	168
Habits, ways of life	34
Cooking	11

5. Text-types

As noted above, my approach to text-types here does not involve the kind of taxonomy one would expect concerning text-types, registers, etc., such as the ones found in Görlach (2004) or Taavitsainen and Pahta (2004). On the contrary, my classification is taken from the one proposed by the compilers of the *Helsinki Corpus*, with some additions of my own. The types considered are set out in Table 5 on the left. The column on the left displays the name of the different text-types, and the one on the right the number of occurrences of Scandinavian loans found for each of the types.

The texts in which Scandinavian terms are used most abundantly are those of a didactic character, among which I have included religious texts, hagiographies, etc.[85] Probably because of this, the number of occurrences of neologisms is so high here, reaching 30.34 % of the total. Texts here include *The Ormulum*, *Fire of Love* by Misyn, *Purity*, *Cursor Mundi*, *The Owl and the Nightingale*, *The Ancrene Riwle* and the different texts of the *Bible*.

The earliest examples, as well as the most numerous, are found in the *Ormulum* from ca. 1200. The terms contained here (as well as the rest of the texts I have checked) are characterised by not being restricted to a particular semantic field. Conversely, I have seen many examples such as (70) below. In this case, the verb (ME *adlen*) is from the semantic field of trade (number 3), and is used here with a figurative sense:

(70) I shall hafenn addledd me Ðe Laferrd Cristess are (Ker 1940)

In a similar way, I have detected some apparently colloquial constructions, such as ME *what have ye ado* meaning "what business is it of yours" where *ado* comes from the ON infinitive *at do(:)*.

(71) Medle nat with that thinge that thu haste nat adoo of (Bühler 1941: 55/11)

I have found terms recorded later that have survived up to the present. Thus, the adjective ME *auk-ward* (in Old Icelandic it is recorded as *ofug-r*) appears around 1400-1425 in *The Pricke of Conscience*:

---

85   It is difficult to separate religious matters from mere didactic texts at the time. For this reason have I chosen to group all these texts under one single category. See Chapter 4.

(72) Đus uses yhong men all new gett, And þe world þai all awkeward set (Morris 1863)

The largest sample of Scandinavian neologisms whose use is clearly figurative appears in the different biblical texts, where parables and other metaphorical structures favour this phenomenon. In example (71) below, taken from the *Sermons of the Gospels,* we can observe how the word ME *bait* (from ON *beita*) belonging to the field of sports and games (number 20) is used to refer to an aspect of everyday life that is moralising due to its comparison with an abstract element:

(73) Cristes godhed the fend tok, Als fisce es tan wit bait and hoe (*Northern Homilies*, Small 1862: 12)

Notwithstanding the abundance of religious texts, other texts, also of a didactic character but with a lower religious and moralising load, are also of interest. This is the case with travelogues. In the following example, from *Mandeville's Travels*, the verb ON *byggja* gives place to ME *biggen* "to build" and is used in the description of a city:

(74) Đis citee es bigge on þe same manere þat Venice es bigged, and þer es þerin xiim brigges and ma (Hamelius 1919: (Eg) 102/6)

The reasons explaining these many cases of Scandinavian elements introduced in medieval didactic texts is that all kinds of borrowings (not only those belonging to a particular field) have been used in these texts. Also, lexical change is already in progress at this stage, so neologisms are adopted and deeply rooted in the linguistic behaviour of most speakers.

As shown in Graph 4 other text-types with an abundance of loans are romance records and minutes, including *Domesday Book*, the *Anglo-Saxon Chronicle*, etc. Among the former, where I have included such notable texts as *The Wars of Alexander*, *Romaunt of the Rose*, *King Horn*, etc., we find examples such as this:

(75) I wol that they togedre go And don al that they han ado (Robinson 1957: 5080)

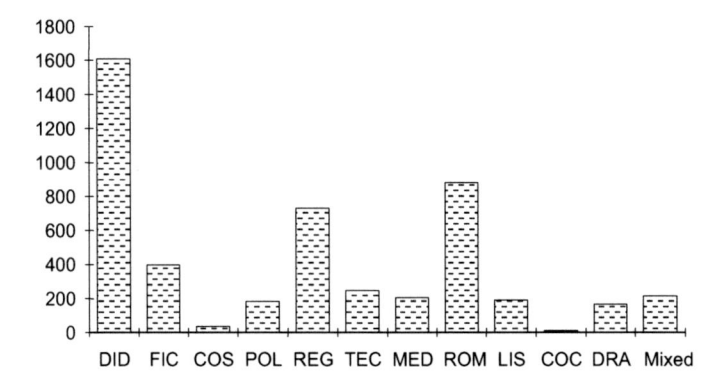

Graph 4: Distribution of loans per text-type.

From records and minutes I have selected an extract from a document referring to the monarchy where the adverb *al-gate* again appears:

(76) O lige lord, þat han bennn plenteuous Vn-to your Liges of your grace algate, Styntith nat now (*Virelai to Henry V for Money*, Furnivall 1892: 18)

Non-religious poetry, as well as fiction, are represented by about 400 tokens each, significantly fewer than didactic texts. All other text types are much lower still. Apart from this, however, and once more returning to the commonly-held view that Scandinavian loans in English are almost completely limited to daily activities, I have checked to what extent this is true of text-types containing neologisms, that is, to what extent texts containing lexical elements taken from Scandinavian languages are those pertaining to everyday life, such as texts on agriculture, country life, etc. Surprisingly, only 11 cases were found in which loans are used in recipe books, such as the ones in Ms Arun. 34, or the fifteenth-century text illustrated below containing the verb *casten*:

(77) Take fayre Flowre & þe whyte of Eyroun [etc.].. þan kaste in a fayre place in þe oven & late bake (Austin 1888)

It should be noted that the number of texts that could be said to be of a technical nature in the corpus is high. Occurrences of loans in purely technical texts number 248, and are found in texts as varied as *Treatise on the Astro-*

labe by Chaucer, *Equatorie of the Planets*, *Medulla Grammatice* or *An Older Form of the Treatyse of Fysshynge with an Angle*. Example (78) has been taken from the last of these, where ME *anger* appears once more:

(78) But the anglear may haue no colde, ne no disese, ne angur, but he be causer hymselfe (Satchell 1883)

On the other hand, there are 206 tokens in medical texts which I had initially included in the count for technical texts but which I finally grouped separately, due to their abundance. These texts include *Medical Works of the Fourteenth Century* (Henslow 1889), the anonymous translation of *Grand Chirurgie* by Guy de Chauliac, and the *Treatises of Fistula in Ano* by John Arderne. This one uses both Latin (no doubt under the influence of its subject-matter) and vernacular terms among which many Scandinavian loans are found:

(79) Puluis sine pari in þis case putte in heleþ wele, bot disesily or angerfully (Power, 1910, 64/30)

An assessment of the text-types where Scandinavian loans appear generally contradicts the widespread idea about the basic, everyday life character of such forms. However, another factor must be taken into consideration: didactic texts are the ones with the highest proportion of loans, and this seems to indicate that such terms are already well-known to the speech community, in that their comprehension seems to have been taken for granted, given that if they were not understood the didactic purpose of the texts would not have been well served.

6. Grammatical categories

A brief review of how Scandinavian loans are distributed across grammatical categories will now be useful. Graph 5 clearly shows the preponderance of verbs (except for gerunds and participles) and nouns over other word-classes.

Verbs represent 40.90% of all the material in my corpus. The most numerous ones (those with a highest number of tokens) are *brennen* (338 tokens), *callen* (168) and, above all, *casten* (with 590). *Casten* and *callen* merit special comment, since their use is very extended use and survives over the centuries with a surprisingly unaltered form, as seen in examples (80) and (81).

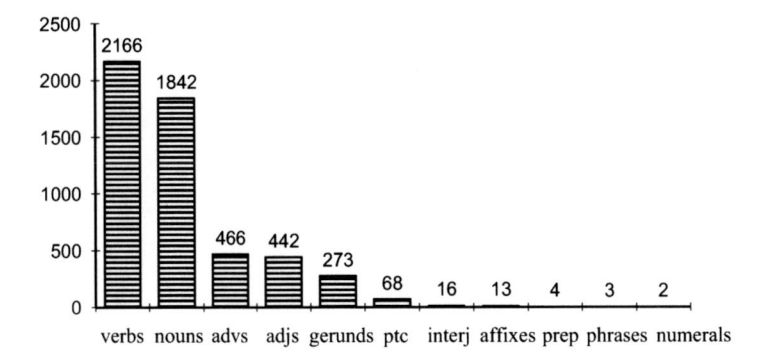

Graph 5. Distribution of loans in grammatical categories

(80) I stod ful stylle and dorste not calle (Gordon 1953)

(81) The Kyng..calt on a maiden (Panton and Donaldson 1869: 388)

As can be observed, the verb resorts to dental suffixes for non-present forms, which is consistent with the acquisition of new verbal forms both in Old and Middle English, since the weak conjugation was the productive one at the time.

The verb *casten* is characterised by its large number of meanings (143 have been collected from the *MED*), although only a few are reproduced in what follows. In (82), the verb means "offer an excuse for delay" and always appears in a legal context:

(82) And ʒif an essoyne be cast [F si tele assoygne seyt jetee] be day of Portmennysmoote be twixene the grete piees, be he aiourned at the next court of Portmennysmoote suyng after (*Ipswich Domesday*, Twiss 1873: (2), 27)

The fragment in (83) is the only instance in the *MED* where *casten* refers to the weather with the meaning of "cause clouds to form"[86]. It appears in a mid thirteenth-century text:

---

86 It should be noted that the term *skies*, also adopted into English, is here used with its original meaning of ON "clouds", which underwent semantic change later, becoming PE "sky".

(83) Ðe ðridde daiges morge quille, ðunder and leuene made spile, On ðis munt stod and skies cast (Morris 1865: 3463)

Table 6.   Distribution of nouns in semantic fields.

SEMANTIC FIELD	TOKENS
01	151
02	9
03	19
04	29
05	84
06	25
07	33
08	107
09	85
10	77
11	174
12	20
13	35
14	92
15	33
16	187
17	23
18	83
19	98
20	31
21	77
22	4
23	7
24	40
25	59
26	5
27	7
28	41
29	18
30	1
31	170
32	12
33	3
34	4
35	1

Following verbs, in terms of frequency, are nouns, representing 34.78% of all grammatical categories. Nouns referring to the semantic field of abstractions constitute the most numerous group, which is perhaps not surprising at all if we bear in mind that abstract entities are often expressed by means of nouns rather than verbs or adjectives.

In addition to the information given in Graph 5, Table 6 on the left provides some details concerning the distribution of the category of noun across the different semantic fields. The left-hand column shows the numbers given to the thirty-five semantic fields under consideration (see Chapter 4) and the column on the right gives the number of noun tokens found for each of those fields.

Some of the nouns referring to abstractions are ME *anger* ("suffering") in (84) and ME *aue* ("danger", "terror") in (85):

(84) He wold neuer play at gamme that was hurt or angre to any man (Mather 1897)

(85) Ðis geant es..of his wordes ful kruell; I sal deliver hir of his aw (Schleich 1887: 2411)

We also have ME *bir(e)* (from ON *byr-r* meaning "favourable wind"), which has an imprecise meaning in ME. In (86) it is used to refer to "a person's strength":

(86) Shippes..ben born aboute of a litel gouernayle, where the bire [WB(2): meuyng; L impetus] of a man dressinge sal wole (Forshall and Madden 1850 Jas.3.4)

Among the least abundant loans, the semantic fields of "place", "position" (number 10) and "quality" (number 35) stand out. There is only one instance of each, reproduced in (87) and (88):

(87) From þe hyest cra vnwarely at onys They fel (Serjeantson 1938)

In (87) the Scandinavian term *kra(:)* appears as ME *cra(:)* "corner, nook", whereas in (88) below, ME *bond* reflects ON *band*, here with the sense of "A force that dominates, controls, compels, constrains, or restrains; domination, dominance, sway", "in confinement, in labor?":

(88) His said wyfe, so beyng but newe in child bed and in the bandes of oure lady, myght not be remeved..withoute jeopardie of hir deth (*Rotuli Parlamentorum; ut et petitiones et placita in parliamento*, 6.52a.)

Table 7. *Distribution of adjectives and adverbs per semantic field*

SEMANTIC FIELD	ADJECTIVE TOKENS	ADVERB TOKENS
01	41	8
02	0	0
03	0	0
04	1	0
05	1	11
06	1	2
07	0	0
08	4	0
09	0	0
10	0	0
11	1	0
12	21	13
13	4	0
14	155	8
15	0	32
16	9	2
17	1	0
18	1	0
19	2	0
20	1	0
21	0	0
22	8	92
23	2	0
24	0	0
25	0	0
26	0	0
27	0	0
28	14	23
29	16	169
30	4	92
31	7	0
32	88	0
33	2	0
34	15	13
35	43	1

Other grammatical categories have an irregular distribution. Adjectives and adverbs represent approximately 8.50%, whereas numerals, prepositions and what Kurath calls 'phrases' barely reach 0.07% of all forms. In order to complete the information provided in Table 6 above, a detailed distribution of adjectives and verbs is offered in Table 7 on the left, in which each of the elements for each of these two categories is assigned to the corresponding semantic fields where they have been found.

The low number of adjectives and adverbs, compared to that of nouns and verbs, may be accounted for by the fact that Old Norse as it was used in England was not regarded as an elegant or literary language, and was in operation in contexts where mere communicative purposes predominated. In general, there is a correspondence between the use of adverbs and adjectives and the type of register to which particular texts belong. Thus, the higher the number of elements belonging to these two word-classes, the more literary or poetic a text tends to be. Roughly speaking, it can be observed that most adjectives and adverbs in English medieval texts have a Norman or Latinate origin. In fact, recent research has shown that nouns are the most numerous word-class in written registers whereas adverbs are more likely to be found in speech (Biber 2006).

Several other significant considerations are worth mentioning in this section. First, as Graph 6 shows, most texts in which Scandinavian loans have been found cannot be safely attributed to a known author and must be considered anonymous.

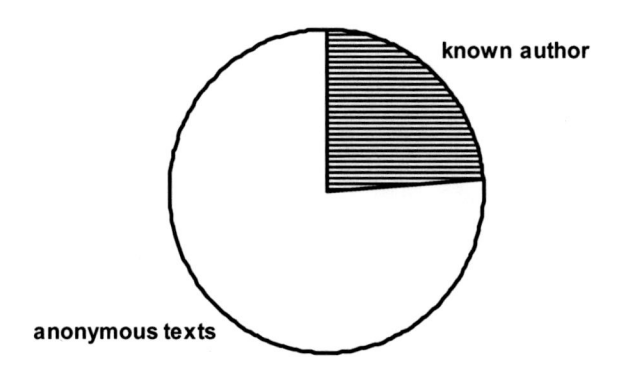

Graph 6.   Authorship of texts

Second, there is a notable difference between the terms gathered by Bjørkman in his classical work (1900-1902) and those that I have scrutinised from my corpus. This may be a crucial factor, in that Bjørkman's work has been used as the essential source for many researchers following him, who in general have not questioned the accuracy of his claims. I have tried to reflect this difference in Graph 7, simply in order to illustrate that other perspectives can be adopted for the study of the influence of Old Norse in English.

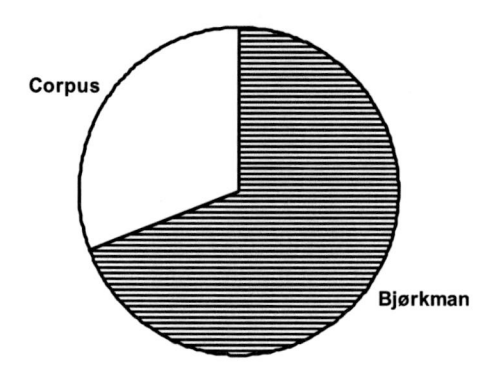

Graph 7.   Scandinavian elements in English not considered by (1900-1902)

Only 3,659 out of the 5,295 forms contained in my corpus were cited by Bjørkman. It must also be pointed out that I refer to tokens, whereas he always referred to types[87]. Therefore, we might perhaps conclude that Bjørkman was not overly concerned with productivity and linguistic habits, and that in this sense my study here is able to provide not only a quantitative approach but also a qualitative analysis of the language reality in Middle English.

---

87   Very illustrative words such as *ay, casten, callen,* etc. may be considered here, where considering tokens would reveal a more extended use.

Chapter Six

Some final remarks

Throughout this study I have tried to focus on the social character of language as a means of communication and to consider that this social nature is an important factor in language change. However, language change is a very broad phenomenon, and for this reason I have limited its scope here. Such a restriction is twofold: first, the time span under analysis has been limited, looking only at Middle English, and assuming a traditional understanding of dates, given that a discussion of the periodisation of the English language is not one of my aims here (Moskowich 2001). Second, I have limited my research to the lexicon.

It is clear that my conception of language as expounded in the current work is far removed from that first posited by Chomsky's (1965) theoretical framework of language, constructed on the notion of an ideal speaker within a homogeneous speech community. On the contrary, my approach attaches great significance to the sociocultural elements in language and, since this study dealt with one particular diachronic development, it also meant that recourse to history was required. When a human being communicates with others, the communicative act takes place in a specific context, and this context determines both the behaviour of speaker and listener, as well as the nature of the message itself. The uses of language are also constrained by certain sociohistorical features. No speaker communicates the same way as another, and even when we refer to a particular stage in the development of a language, rather than to individuals, we must bear in mind that such stages may be anything but uniform, as well as differing greatly from the ones preceding and following them. The study of the history of English, or indeed any language, as a succession of linguistic phenomena must be regarded as a mere pedagogical tool.

I consider, then, that sociolinguistic studies must be carried out to determine the kinds of relations established among speakers and, consequently, among the users of different codes or varieties. The usefulness of sociolinguistics increases when there is a goal beyond the relationship between the high and low varieties of a given language and when two or more languages are contemplated as they interact. It is at this point that the analysis of the type of communities involved becomes necessary, as a means of ascertaining which language is used for each kind of intercourse (if specific linguistic habits do indeed correspond to specific communicative contexts). When analysing Scandinavian loans in English from this perspective, then, I have first dealt with the social and historical context of Scandinavian England, focusing on the Danelaw, since it was the area most heavily settled by the Norse. Because I have chosen a view of language and society as a single structured entity, some knowledge of the social organisation of the Danelaw and the historical process leading to its formation contribute to an understanding of the linguistic phenomena occurring there, including lexical change. Indeed, when observing the contact of Old English and the Scandinavian languages (mainly, Danish) in a situation which is not entirely uniform, I have tried to account for the behaviour that might have led to some forms surviving while others were lost forever. In so doing I have concentrated on lexical issues and have only mentioned in passing that which may have occurred in the field of grammar. Therefore, discussions on word-order (Pintzuk 2002), pronouns (Morse Gagne 1988; Ritt 2001), the form and use of prepositions (Krygier 2011; Iglesias Rábade 2011) or of phrasal verbs (Malak 2010) have not been dealt with.

The study of English borrowing from Old Norse was initiated by Erik Bjørkman in the early twentieth century. Since then, other authors have followed his line of research although, unfortunately, the ensuing studies were often mere lists of words with a Scandinavian etymological origin found or used in each of the periods of English. All of them, however, have tried to offer a historical introduction, although none seems to have made deep connections between history and society and the evolution of the language. Thus, my intention was to offer a more complete account of a well-known although not satisfactorily explained phenomenon; such an account necessitated a detailed analysis of the socio-historical context as a starting point.

After analysing the historical circumstances of the arrival of the Scandinavian peoples in England in the tenth century, it can be affirmed that, contrary to the generally accepted idea that the Vikings (as a synonym of pirates) were responsible for the raiding of England, the Scandinavians were certainly not all Vikings in this sense. Historical evidence seems to indicate that the Scandinavian invasion was in fact more of a colonisation. Whereas two centuries later the Normans would get rid of the local nobility and clergy, replacing them with their own barons and bishops, there is no evidence that the Danes did anything similar. Theirs was not an aristocratic conquest but a national migration with no intention to dispossess the native Anglo-Saxons. Rather, they settled on land that the natives were not exploiting. I do not suggest that no violence occurred over the course of the whole process, and it may not have been very different from the process found in other areas and with other peoples, including the Anglo-Saxons themselves (and the Romans before them) in their behaviour towards the native Celtic tribes.

Besides the information from sources such as the *Anglosaxon Chronicle* and certain sagas, I have resorted to placenames. These testify to the number of settlements the Danes founded in England, but also help us understand what type of settlements these were. Placenames have sometimes been used to assess what kind of relationship one settlement had with another (small villages depending on larger ones, farms selling their products to nearby towns, walled cities protecting neighbouring hamlets, etc.).

The study of the historical process culminating with the Scandinavian colonisation of England in two successive waves led almost inevitably to a detailed exploration of the organisation of the newcomers' communities. I have also found it useful to ascertain whether many differences existed between this social structure in the Danelaw and in the rest of the English territory, where the Scandinavian proportion of the population seems to have been clearly inferior. Such a social fabric, so different from the one the Danes found when they arrived in the British Isles, must also have led to a modification in linguistic habits, if we accept the concept of language as a social fact.

In principle, the data available does not seem to suggest that the coming of these new settlers implied the imposition of a different sociocultural framework on the native one. It is more a gradual assimilation process. Hence, the study of the social hierarchies of the communities may better lead us to know the nature of speech communities and what kind of behaviour could have been expected from speakers in each community depending on their situation in the social scale.

Such a sociocultural amalgam is notably enhanced from 1066 when the Normans (also of Scandinavian descent) arrived in England with the intention of ruling over it. The inhabitants of England united against the common enemy, doing so without considering whether they were of Anglo-Saxon or

Scandinavian extraction. In my view, this association may have had significant linguistic consequences, for example, in the fact that the number of loans recorded from the eleventh century is higher than it had ever been before.

The election of the *Middle English Dictionary* for my corpus is due to its reliability. It is precisely the breadth of the information it contains what allows for extensive searches for examples, since it contains a very high number of texts of very different types. The variety of text-types represented facilitates the analysis not only of diatopic stratification, but also of stylistic stratification as these affect the distribution of Scandinavian loanwords in English.

A revision of the three most relevant sociolinguistic models made it clear that none of them alone was wholly applicable to this study, due to the amount and nature of the historical, social and linguistic data available. The study of variation proposed by Labov advocates the existence of diverse variants or forms of the same linguistic item. In general, variation studies following Labov's line of research have focused on phonological variants, since they based their work on oral data. The information gathered is then processed according to different variables, such as sex, age, cultural level and the contexts in which the information has been obtained (whether it is an informal conversation, reading isolated words or fragments, etc).

Clearly, this type of study brings with it certain limitations due to the way in which the information is obtained. However, it also defines concepts that are basic for the understanding of language as the manifestation of a particular sociohistorical reality, such concepts as "variant" and "social stratification", "stylistic stratification", etc., concepts also central to the more general study of variation. Although in this particular study mathematical quantification and processing of the information is not possible to any great extent, I can affirm that variation must have existed. In this sense the Labovians provide a wonderful opportunity to explain language change by adding to the intra-systemic reasons certain concepts and processes in which variation is involved. In this way, lexical change may be explained by the selection of a Scandinavian term instead of an Anglo-Saxon one, both being considered variants within a variable. When two forms co-vary they are not usually precisely the same, but rather one or the other carries some type of added information or social connotation. In Labov's theory some variant forms are said to be stigmatised. In the case of Anglo-Norse, Scandinavian origin forms were stigmatised too, at least at the beginning, and only slowly became unmarked as their use spread. Such variants are unmarked only when they lose the social load they had and do not convey any social meaning to the listener. At this point, both the Scandinavian and the Anglo-Saxon forms coexist, until one of them acquires a new stigma and its use is restricted to a particular group, or shifts its meaning, or indeed simply disappears.

Milroy's approach to the question of social networks led me to focus on the concept of speech community and to look closely at its different definitions. Sure enough, this model provides a very definite vision of how speech communities are structured depending on the socio-economical ties existing between the members of a speech community. Milroy proposes that the tighter the ties and the more numerous the relations within a community, the closer it will be (high density network) and, therefore, the less likely it will be to undergo any kind of external influence. Of course, among the possible linguistic influences here are those favouring language change. However, if a community is relatively open to relations with members of other communities, the network is considered of low density. Also, if relations, both within and between communities, are maintained across different settings or spheres of life, then influences from surrounding networks are more likely to penetrate.

This model, I believe, is of great use when looking at communities existing in the past, although it has the drawback of not being equally effective when applied to small networks of which we have a limited knowledge. This is the case with those communities that may have existed in the Danelaw, the information about which is available only through records, minutes and charts. In fact, information on social life in the Danelaw is limited to how it was organised from an economic perspective (land management in a rural society) and how, depending on this type of economy, different social groups were established, the most numerous of which were the *ceorles* in their different sub-classes (*geneat, gebur* and *cotsetla*). In cases like the one under study here, the value of Milroy's model is to be found in that, together with a Labovian explanation of language change, it helps us explain what might have happened in Northeastern England ten centuries ago. Thus, although we cannot reconstruct a particular social network in all its detail, we can imagine the kind of average community and its activities. From this knowledge we can go on to consider the language register (including vocabulary) that its speakers may have used. If, in addition, we consider the issue of whether Anglo-Saxon speakers interacted with Scandinavian speakers from other communities or those within the same community, we might hypothesise that certain lexical elements would have become variants that could have co-existed for a certain length of time. In such cases, the Scandinavian form would surely be marked at the beginning as a foreign loan, and following this the process described above would then have developed.

Both theories are in this sense complementary. In fact, according to the historical details provided here, it is possible that relations between Danes and English became more necessary and hence tighter from the time of the Norman Conquest. This seems to be confirmed by my analysis, with a higher number of loans from the moment the Normans arrived, this, of course, being the case in the geographical area where the presence of Scandinavians was high.

Finally, Bailey's theory provides a model of language change as a phenomenon within the field of diachrony and, as such, it contemplates time as a fundamental factor in addition to those that had usually been taken into consideration in this type of study. Notwithstanding, Bailey's model on its own cannot be applied to the linguistic situation of this particular study. As with the other two frameworks discussed, it must be used together with other approaches. Indeed, none of the three can be used in isolation in the case of Anglonorse, although they have all been useful for my research.

My analysis has also shed some light on another, more specific aspect of the phenomenon which deserves some attention. Contrary to what is generally believed, Scandinavian loans in English, even in Old English, and more so as time goes by, are not limited in their use, either to certain semantic fields or to particular dialects. It has often been claimed (Bjørkman 1902; Serjeantson 1935; Geipel 1971) that such loans in English refer to everyday life, and their supposed restricted semantic scope has often been compared to that of French borrowings (usually defined as restricted semantic fields and denoting a higher socio-cultural level).

However, a thorough semantic classification of the use of tokens in my corpus, in contrast to the classification of types of preceding studies, provided more accurate, concrete evidence here, and hence it was possible to affirm that Scandinavian loans are more frequent in the common core vocabulary than in any specific lexical field, be it daily life, agriculture, seafaring, etc. In fact, I have detected a great abundance of terms referring to human experience, both physical and mental. On these lines, then, it is worth mentioning that although the first dialects affected by this lexical change were those in the North and East, most loans have until now been counted in the standard or unmarked variety.

If we accept that bilingualism is a phenomenon implying identical competence in two languages and the wholly interchangeable use of both, we must assume the Anglo-Norse society in the Middle Ages was probably not bilingual from a collective or societal point of view. I would prefer to consider bilingualism as an individual phenomenon, and in this sense communities can be said to have been diglossic to a greater or lesser degree.

The study of social networks and the consideration in parallel of socio-historical and linguistic information have allowed me to reconstruct to a certain extent the kind of linguistic behaviour that the inhabitants of England might have had at this time. Taking into account both social and cultural contexts, these speakers may be said to have exhibited linguistic behaviour typical of low level cultural groups in communities with two languages. That is, they may have exhibited primary semibilingualism, given that they knew the low variety of both languages but probably not, considering the degree of literacy at the time, the high varieties. The very close co-existence of two languages whose grammatical system was virtually the same may in some way have meant that the average speaker overcame any elements which might have interfered with communication, so vital for social and economic reasons.

Whatever peculiarities the socio-cultural setting contribute to a language, in the sense that language is a social fact and is bound to reflect such peculiarities, these peculiarities are extremely relevant for the study of its historical development. When one single geographical space embraces two languages, it also embraces two cultural realities. Both languages exist independently until the moment at which the social and cultural interchange is such that spontaneous speech innovations occur (Vann 2009), and the existence of two separate linguistic codes becomes unnecessary to refer to what is in effect a new, single reality. Thus, when the Anglo-Saxon and Scandinavian societies became one, particularly after the Norman Conquest, the two languages that had once been spoken gave rise to what we know today as English.

Appendix

Abreviations of cited texts and manuscripts

* References to titles and incipits have not been included here due to their extension. For further details, see Kurath et al. (eds.) (1956-1963: 23-105).

1.Manuscripts and manuscript collections

Acland-Hood	Sir Alexander Acland-Hood, formerly.
Add	British Museum, Additional.
Adv	Advocates Library, Edinburgh.
Aldh	Lord Aldenham (= Sir Henry Gibbs), formerly.
Antq	Society of Antiquaries, London.
Arms	College of Arms (including a group of Arundel MSS).
Army	Army Medical Library, Washington.
Arun	British Museum, Arundel.
AS	All Soul's College, Oxford.
Ashb	Ashburnham, formerly.
Ashm	Bodleian Library, Ashmole.
Auch	Auchinleck MS (= Adv 19.2.1, with fragments in Ednb-U 218).
Aug	British Museum, Cotton Augustus.
Bal	Balliol College, Oxford.
Barl	Bodleian Library, Barlow.
Bedf	Bedford MS (= Add 36983).
Bil	Billyng MS, present location unknown.
Bod	Bodleian Library, Bodley.
BodAdd	Bodleian Library, Additional.
BodeMus	Bodleian Library, e Museo.
BodKCh	Bodleian Library, Kent Charters.
BodLTh	Bodleian Library, Latin Theology.
BodLtrg	Bodleian Library, Liturgy.
BodPoet	Bodleian Library, Engl. Poet.
BodR	Bodleian Library, Bodley Rolls.
BodTh	Bodleian Library, English Theology.
Bridg	Bridgwater Corporation.
Brist-U	University of Bristol.
Brm	Boke of Brome, formerly at Brome Hall.
Brsn	Brasenose College, Oxford.
Brussels	Royal Library, Brussels.
Burton	Preb. John R. Burton.
Butler-Bowdon	Col. Butler-Bowdon.
Cai	Gonville & Caius College, Cambridge.
Calth	Lord Calthorpe (= Yelverton).
Carla	Earl of Carlisle (formerly at Castle Howard).
CC	Christ Church College, Oxford.
Chal	Challoner MS, present ownership unknown.
Chet	Chetham Library, Manchester.
ChrC-Dub	Christ Church, Dublin.
ChU	University of Chicago.
Cld	British Museum, Cotton Claudius.

Cleo	British Museum, Cotton Cleopatra.
Clg	British Museum, Cotton Caligula.
Cmb	Cambridge University Library.
Cnt	Canterbury Cathedral.
Copenh	Royal Library, Copenhagen.
Corp-C	Corpus Christi College, Cambridge.
Corp-O	Corpus Christi College, Oxford.
CotApp	British Museum, Cotton Appendix.
CotR	British Museum, Cotton Rolls.
Cuth	St. Cuthbert's College, Durham.
Davies	John Speed Davies, formerly.
Dc	Bodleian Library, Douce.
Delam	Delamere MS (= Vale Royal MS = Penrose 10).
Deritend	Deritend House, formerly.
Dewick	Dewick MS (= Brighton MS), present ownership unknown.
Dgb	Bodleian Library, Digby.
Dlw	Dulwich College, London.
Dom	British Museum, Cotton Domitian.
Dub	Trinity College, Dublin.
Dun	Dunrobin MS.
Dur-C	Durham Cathedral.
Dur-Ex	Durham, Exchequer.
Dur-U	Durham University.
Ednb-U	University of Edinburgh.
Eg	British Museum, Egerton.
Elsm	Ellesmere MS (= Hnt EL 26.C.9).
Em	Emmanuel College, Cambridge.
Erf	Royal Library, Erfurt.
Eton	Eton College.
Ex	Exeter (city).
Fenn	Fenn MS, present ownership unknown.
Fil	Fillingham MS (= Add 37492).
Fitzw	Fitzwilliam MS, present ownership unknown.
Folg	Folger Shakespeare Memorial Library.
Fountains	Fountains Abbey, orig.
Frf	Bodleian Library, Fairfax.
Fst	British Museum, Cotton Faustina.
Gar	Princeton University, Garrett.
Ghent	University Library, Ghent.
Glb	British Museum, Cotton Galba.
Gldh	Guildhall Library, London.
Got	University Library, Gottingen.
Gough	Bodleian Library, Gough.
Graham	Sir Richard Graham.
Gren	Library, Grenoble.
GrI	Gray's lnn.
Grv	Bodleian Library, Greaves.
Gurn	J. H. Gurney, formerly.
Hal	J. O. Halliwell, formerly.
Harv	Harvard University.
Hat	Bodleian Library, Hatton.
Hatfield	Hatfield House, MSS of Marquis of Salisbury.
Helm	Helmingham Hall, MSS of Lord Tollemache.
Heng	Henwrt Ms of Chaucer CT (= Pen 392D).

Appendix

Henslow	J. G. Henslow, formerly.
Hlk	Holkham Hall, MSS of Earl of Leicester.
Hnt	Huntington Library.
Hrf-C	Hereford Cathedral.
Hrl	British Museum, Harley.
Htrn	Hunterian Museum, Glasgow.
Huth	Alfred Huth, formerly.
Ing	Sir Henry Ingilby, formerly.
IrBl	Ireland-Blackburn MS (= Hale Hall MS).
Jas	Bodleian Library, James.
Jes-C	Jesus College, Cambridge.
Jes-O	Jesus College, Oxford.
Jul	British Museum, Cotton Julius.
Jun	Bodleain Library, Junius.
KC	King's College, Cambridge.
Kil	Kilkenny Castle, Ormond.
Lamb	Lambeth Palace.
Lawson	Sir John Lawson, formerly.
Ld	Bodleian Library, Laud.
Leyden	University Library, Leyden.
Lin-C	Lincoln Cathedral.
LinI	Lincoln's Inn.
Lnsd	British Museum, Landsdowne.
Magd-C	Magdalen College, Cambridge.
Magd-O	Magdalen College, Oxford.
Marl	Marlborough Vicarage.
Mayer	Joseph Mayer, formerly.
McM	Fitzwilliam Museum, McClean.
Mdst	Maidstone Museum, Kent.
Med-L	Medical Society, London.
Mert	Merton College, Oxford.
Mid	Lord Middleton (formerly at Wollaton Hall).
Min-U	University of Minnesota.
Monson	Lord Monson.
Most	Lord Mostyn, formerly.
Mrg	J. Plerpont Morgan Library, New York.
MSC	Michigan State College.
Naples	Royal National Library, Naples.
NC	New College, Oxford.
Nero	British Museum, Cotton Nero.
Nthld	Duke of Northumberland.
Nwb	Newberry Library, Chicago.
Nwnh	Newnham College, Cambridge.
NY	New York Academy of Medicine.
Otho	British Museum, Cotton Otho.
Paris	Bibliothèque Nationale, Paris.
Pavia	University Library, Pavia.
Payne	Payne MS, present location unknown.
Pen	Mrs. Wynn, Peniarth, Wales (on deposit at the national Library, Wales; formerly Hengwrt).
Pep	Pepys, Magdalen College, Cambridge.
Peterb	Peterborough Cathedral.
Peterh	Peterhouse, Cambridge.
Petw	Petworth, MSS of Lord Leconfield.

Petyt	Petyt, Inner Temple Library.
Phil	Sir Thomas Phillipps, formerly.
Phys-E	Royal College of Physicians, Edinburgh.
Phys-L	Royal College of Physicians, London.
Pmb-C	Pembroke College, Cambridge.
Pmb-O	Pembroke College, Oxford.
Porter	Porter MS, present location unknown.
Pratt	Lt. Col. Edward Pratt, formerly.
Prk	Porkington (on deposit at the National Library, Wales).
PRO	Public Record Office.
Qu-C	Queen's College, Cambridge.
Qu-O	Queen's College, Oxford.
RBOss	Red Book of Ossory.
Rob	Viscount Clifden, Lord Robartes.
Roy	British Museum, Royal.
Rsnb	A. S. W. Rosenbach, New York.
Rwl	Bodleain Library, Rawlinson.
Ryl	John Rylands Library, Manchester.
Sal	Salisbury Cathedral.
SAsht	Steeple Ashton Vicarage.
Seld	Bodleian Library, Selden.
Selw	Selwyn College.
Seton	Walter W. Seton (= Pennant MS).
Shrw	Shrewsbury School.
Sid	Sidney Sussex College, Cambridge.
Sim	Simeon MS (= Add 22283).
Sln	British Museum, Sloane.
StJ-C	St. John's College, Cambridge.
StJ-O	St. John's College, Oxford.
Stnh	Stonyhurst College.
Stockh	Royal Library, Stockholm.
StP	St. Paul's Cathedral.
Stw	British Museum, Stowe.
Suth	Sutherland MS (= Eg 2862).
Tan	Bodleian Library, Tanner.
Tbr	British Museum, Cotton Tiberius.
TH	Trinity Hall, Cambridge.
Thrn	Thornton MS (= Lin-C 91).
Tit	British Museum, Cotton Titus.
Tol	Tollemache Ms of Trev. Barth., now Mrg.
Trentham	Trentham Hall, MSS of Duke of Sutherland.
Trin-C	Trinity College, Cambridge.
Trin-O	Trinity College, Oxford.
UC	University College, Oxford.
Vit	British Museum, Cotton Vitellius.
Vrn	Vernon MS (= BodPoet A.1).
Vsp	British Museum, Cotton Vespasian.
Way	A. Way, formerly.
Wel	Wellcome Foundation Library, London.
Whitchurch	Free Library, Whitchurch, Shropshire.
Wht	Wheatley MS (= Add 39574).
Win	Winchester Cathedral.
Win-C	Winchester College.
Win-Gidh	Winchester, Guildhall.

Wor	Worcester Cathedral.
Yk-M	York Minster.

2. Periodicals, series and Festschriften

AAHSCJ	Architectural, Archaelogical and Historic Society of Chesire: Journal (Chester 1857-).
AASRP	Associated Architectural Societies: Reports and papers (London 1851-).
AB	Altenglische Bibliothek, ed. E. Kölbing (Heilbronn 1883-90).
AC	Abbotsford Club. Publications (Edinburgh 1835-65).
AIGBI	Royal Archeological Institute of Great Britain and Ireland: Journal (London 1845-).
AJP	American Journal of Philology (Baltimore 1880-).
AMT	Alt- und mittelenglische Texte, ed. L. Morsbach and F. Holthausen (Heidelberg 1901).
Anc.	The Ancestor: Review of county & family history, heraldry & antiquities (London 1902).
Anec.O.	Anecdota Oxiniensia: Texts, documents & extracts, chiefly from manuscripts in the Bodleian and other Oxford libraries: Mediaeval series (Oxford 1882-1914).
Anglia	Anglia: Zeitschrift für englische Philologie (Halle 1877-).
Anglia B.	Anglia Beiblatt: Mitteilungen über englische Sprache, etc. (Halle 1891-).
Antiq.	The Antiquary: Magazine devoted to the study of the past (London, 1880-1915).
Ant. J.	Antiquaries Journal: Society of antiquaries (London 1921).
APKittredge	Anniversary Papers by Colleagues and Pupils of George Lyman Kittredge (Boston 1913).
AQC	Ars Quatour Coronatorum: Transactions of the Quatour coronati lodge no. 2076, London (Margate 1888-).
Archaeol.	Archaeologia: Tracts relating to antiquity, Society of antiquaries of London (London 1770-).
Archaeol. Ael.	Archaeologia Aeliana: Tracts relating to antiquities, Society of antiquaries of Newcastle-upon-Tyne (Newcastle 1822-).
Archaeol. Cant.	Archaeologia Cantiana: Transactions of the Kent archaeologial society (London 1858-).
Archaeol. J.	The Archaeological Journal: Royal archaeological institute of Great Britain and Ireland, (London 1844).
Archiv	Archiv für das Studium der neuren Sprachen und Literaturen (1846-).
BAAJ	British Archaeological Association: Journal (London 1846-).
BAP	Bibliothek der angelsächsischen Prosa, ed. Grein & Wulker (1872-).
BARSEHEW	British Academy: Records of the social and economic history of England and Wales (London 1914-).
BBA	Bonner Beiträge zur Anglistik, ed. M. Trautmann (Bonn 1898-1908).
BBGRP	Berliner Beiträge zur germanischen und romanischen Philologie, ed. Ebering (Berlin 1893-).
BBOAJ	Berks., Bucks. and Oxon. Archaeological Journal (reading 1895-).
BC	Bannatyne Club: Publications (Edinburgh 1823-75).
Bdf: HRS	Bedfordshire Historical Record Society: Publications (1913-).
Bdf. NQ	Bedfordshire Notes and Queries (1886-93).
BGAS	Bristol and Gloucestershire Archaeological Society: Transactions (Gloucester 1876-).

Appendix

BMQ	The British Museum Quarterly (London 1927-).
BQR	The Bodleian Quarterly Record (Oxford 1914-1938).
BREPFF	Beitrage zur romanischen und englischen Philologie: Festgabe für Wendelin Foerster (Halle 1902).
Bristol RS	Bristol Record Society: Publications (Bristol 1930).
Britannica	Britannica: Max Forster zum sechzigsten Geburtstage (Leipzig, 1929).
BRS	British Record Society, limited: The index library, containing indexes, calendars, and abstracts of British records (London 1888-).
BSEP	Bonner studien zur englischen Philologie (Bonn 1909-).
Bull. IHR	Institute of Historical Research, London University: Bulletin (London 1923).
Bull. MHRA	Modern Humanities Research Association: Bulletin (Cambridge 1919-).
Bull. RL	Rylands Library Bulletin.
Bull. WR	The Western Reserve University Bulletin (Cleveland 1895).
Camd.	Camden Society: Royal Historical Society, London: Publications, Camden series (London 1838-1901).
Cant. Yk. S	Canterbury and York Society: Publications (London 1905-).
Chet.	Chetham Society: Remains, historical & literary.. of Lancaster and Chester (Manchester 1844-88).
Chs. Sheaf	The Cheshire Sheaf (Chester 1880-).
Cmb. AC	Cambridge Antiquarian Society: Communications (Cambridge 1859-91).
Cmb. AS	Cambridge Antiquarian Society; Publications (Cambridge, v.d.).
CS	Chaucer Society: Publications (London 1868-).
Cum. West. AS	Cumberland and Westmoreland Antiquarian and Archeological Society: Transactions (Kendal 1874-).
Der. ANHSJ	Derbyshire Archeological and Natural History Society: Journal (London 1879-).
Dev. Cor. NQ	Devon and Cornwall Notes and Queries: Journal (Exeter 1901).
Disc.	Discovery: Journal of knowledge (Cambridge 1920-).
Dugd. Soc.	Dugdale Society: Publications (Oxford 1921-).
EAS Brown	Essays & Studies in Honour of Carleton Brown (New York 1940).
EB	Erlanger Beiträge zur englischen Philologie und vergleichenden Litteraturgeschichte, ed. H. Varnhagen (Erlangen 1889-1904).
EDS	English Dialect Society: Publications (London 1873-1896).
EETS	Early English Text Society, original series (London 1864-).
EETSAS	Early English Text Society, Advanced Specimens.
EETSES	Early English Text Society, Extra Series (London 1867-).
EGSt.	English and Germanic Studies (Birmingham 1947-).
EHR	The English Historical Review (London 1886-).
EJ	The English Journal: Organ of the national council of teachers of English. (Chicago 1912-).
EMisc. Furnivall	An English Miscellany, Presented to Dr. Furnivall (Oxford 1901).
EPNS	English Place-Name Society: Publications (Cambridge 1924-).
Ess. AST	Essex Archaeological Society: Transactions (Colchester 1858-).
ESt.	Englische Studien: Organ fur englische philologie (Heilbronn, Leipzig 1877-).
EStudies	English Studies: Jounal of English letters and philology, (Amsterdam 1919-).
ESUM	Essays ans Studies in English and Comparative Literature, University of Michigan (Ann Arbor 1925-).
ESUU	Essays and Studies in English and Comparative Literature, Upsala University (Upsala 1949-).
ET	Englische Textbibliothek, ed.J. Hoops ((Heidelberg 1898-).
Fenland NQ	Fenland Notes and Queries: Journal (Peterborough 1891-1909).
Fest. NM	Festschrift zum 12. Neuphilologentage in München (Eralangen 1906).
GRM	Germanisch-Romanische Monatsschrift (Heidelberg,1909-).

Hak.Soc.	Hakluyt Society, Works issued by (London 1847-).
Hamp. RS	Hampshire Record Society: Publications (London 1889-99).
HBS	Henry Bradshaw Society: Publications (London 1891-).
HES	Harvard Economic Studies (Boston 1906-).
HHS	Harvard Historical Studies (New York 1896-).
Hist.	History: Journal of the Historical Association (London 1912-).
HLQ	Huntington Library Quarterly (San Marino, Calif. 1937-).
HMC Rep.	Historical Manuscripts Commission: Reports (London 1870-).
HMC Var. Col.	Historical Manuscripts Commission: Report on manuscripts in various collections (London 1901-14).
Hrl. Soc.	Harleian Society: Publications (London 1869-).
HSLC	Historic Society of Lancashire and Cheshire: Transactions (Liverpool, 1848-).
HSNPL	Harvard Studies and Notes in Philology and Literature (Cambridge 1892-).
IF	Indogermanische Forschungen: Zeitschrift fur Indogermanistik (Berlin 1891-).
JEGP	Journal of English and Germanic Philology (Urbana, Ill. 1897-).
JP	Jahrbuch für Philologie = Idealistische Philologie (Munich 1925-).
JRESL	Jahrbuch für romanische und englische Sprache und Literatur (Berlin 1859-).
JRLB	John Rylands Library: Bulletin (Manchester 1903-).
KAA	Kölner anglistische Arbeiten (Leipzig 1927-).
Kaiserl. Akad.	Kaiserliche Akademie der Wissenschaften: Sitzungsberichte (Berlin 1882-).
LAAS	Leicestershire Architectural and Archeological Society: Reports ans papers (Leicester 1855-).
Lang.	Language: Journal of the Linguistic Society of America (Baltimore 1925-).
LCAS	Lancashire and Cheshire Antiquarian Society: Transactions (Manchester 1884-).
LCRS	Lancashire and Cheshire Record Society: Publications (London, 1879-).
LG	Local Gleanings: Magazine, chiefly relating to Lancashire and Cheshire (Manchester 1879-80).
LGRP	Literaturblatt für germanische und romanische Philologie (Heilbronn, 1880-1944).
Library	The Library: Quarterly review of bibLiography (London 1889-).
Lin. NQ	Lincolnshire Notes and Queries: Journal (Horncastle 1888-).
Lin. RS	Lincoln Record Society: Publications (Lincoln 1911-).
LMS	London Mediaeval Studies (London 1937-).
LS	Loomis Studies: Medieval Studies in memory of Gertrude Schoepperle Loomis (Paris 1927).
LSE	Leeds Studies in English and kindred languages (Leeds 1932-).
LSELTM	Leeds University, School of English Language: Texts & Monographs (Kendal 1935-).
LuSE	Lund Studies in English (Lund 1933-).
MA	Medium Ævum: Organ of the Society for the study of mediaeval languages and literature (Oxford 1932-).
MB	Münchener Beiträge zur romanischen und englischen Philologie (Erlangen, Leipzig 1890-).
MHS	University of Manchester Publications: Historical series (Manchester 1904-).
MLJ	The Modem Language Joumal (Menasha, Wis., 9116-).
MLN	Modern Language Notes (Baltimore 1886-).
MLQ	Modern Langauge Quarterly (London 1897-1904).
MLR	The Modern Language Review: Devoted to the study of medieval and modern literature (Cambridge 1905-).

MP	Modern Philology: Journal devoted to research in modern languages and literatures (Chicago 1903-).
MSoc. S	Malone Society: Studies (London v.d.).
Neb. St.	University of Nebraska Studies in the humanities (Lincoln 1941-).
New Shak. Soc.	New Shakspere Society: Publications (London 1874-92).
NM	Neuphilologische Mitteilungen (Helsingfors 1889-).
North. RS	Northamptonshire Record Society: Publications (Hereford, Kettering 1920-).
NPalaeog. Soc.	New Paleographical Society: Facsimiles of ancient manuscripts (London 1903-12).
NQ Ser.	Notes and Queries: Medium of intercommunication for literary men (London 1849-).
Nrf. Antiq. Misc.	The Norfolk Antiquarian Miscellany (Norwich 1877-1908).
Nrf. Archaeol.	Norfolk Archaeology: Tracts (Norwich 1847-).
NRS	Navy Records Society: Publications (London 1894-).
OAST	Oxfordshire Archaeological Society: Transactions (Banbury 1856-).
OHS	Oxford Historical Society: Publications (Oxford,1884-).
OJGBI	Obsterical Journal of Great Britain and Ireland (Philadelphia 1873-80).
ORS	Oxford Records Society: Record series (Oxford 1919-).
Osiris	Osiris: Studies of the history and philosophy of science, etc. (Bruges 1936-).
OSSLH	Oxford Studies in Social and Legal History, ed. P. Vinogradoff (Oxford 1909-27).
Palaeog. Soc.	Paleographical society: Facsimiles of manuscripts and inscriptions (London 1873-83).
PCmb. AS	Cambridge Antiquarian Society: Communications and Proceedings (Cambridge 1859-).
Pipe R. Soc.	Pipe Roll Society: Publications (London 1884-).
PLPLSoc.	Leeds Philosophical and Literary Society: Proceedings, literary and historical section (Leeds 1925-).
PMLA	Modern Lang. Association of America: Publications (Baltimore, Menasha 1884-).
PQ	Philological Quarterly (Iowa City 1922-).
PRIA	Royal Irish Academy: Proceedings (Dublin 1841-).
PRSM	Royal Society of Medicine: Proceedings (London,1907-).
PS	Percy Society: Publications (London 1840-52).
PSAL	Society of Antiquaries of London: Proceedings (London 1843-, also sposonsored publications 1787; 1790).
PST	Philological Society: Transactions (London 1854-).
QF	Quellen und Forschungen zur Sprach - und Kultur- geschichteder germanischen Völker. (Strassburg 1874-1918).
RC	Roxburghe Club: Publications (London 1814-).
Reliq.	The Reliquary and Illustrated Archaeologist: Devoted to the study of the early pagan and Christian antiquities of Great Britain (London 1860-1909).
RES	Review of English Studies: Journal of English literature and the English language (London 1925-).
RHS	Royal Historical Society: Publications (London 1838-).
Romania	Romania: Recueil..consacré a l'étude des langues et des littératures romanes (Paris 1872-).
RR	Romanic Review: Journal devoted to research..in the field of the Romance languages and literatures (New York 1910-).
RS	Rolls Series: Rerum britannicarum medii aevi scriptores (London 1858-96).
RSLT	Royal Soceity of Literature of the United Kingdom: Transactions (London 1829-).
SAC	Surrey Archaeological Society: Collections (London 1858-).
Salop. SP	Salopian Shreds and Patches (Shrewsbury 1874-91).

Appendix

SANHS	Somersetshire Archaeol. and Natural History Society: Proceedings (Taunton 1849-).
SANT	Society of Antiquaries of Newcastle upon Tyne: Proceedings (Newcastle 1855-).
STAF	Société des Anciens Textes Francais: Publications (Paris, v.d.).
SEEP	Select Early English Poems, ed. Sir I. Gollancz (London 1913-).
Seld. Soc.	Selden Society: Publications (London 1887-).
SEP Klaeber	Studies in English philology in honor of Frederick Klaeber, ed. K. Malone & M.B.Ruud (Minneapolis 1929).
Shake. Soc.	Shakespeare Society: Publications (London 1853-).
SIANH	Suffolk Institute of Archaeology and Natural History: Proceedings (Bury St. Edmunds 1853-).
Som. Dor. NQ	Somerset and Dorset Notes and Queries (Sherborne 1890-).
Som. RS	Somerset Record Society: Publications (London 1887-).
Sou. RS	Soutahmpton Record Society: Publications (Southampton 1905-).
SP	Studies in Philology (Chapel Hill, N.C. 1906-).
Spec.	Speculum: Journal of mediaeval studies (Cambridge, Mass. 1926-).
SSML	Smith College Studies in Modern Languages (Northampton 1919-).
ST. Paul Eccl. Soc.	St. Paul's Ecclesiological Society: Transactions (London 1879-1937).
STS	Scottish Text Society: Publications (Edinburgh 1884-).
Suf. GB	Suffolk Green Books, ed. S.H.A. Hervey (Woodbridge 1894-1929).
Sur. Soc.	Surtees Society: Publications (Durham 1835-).
Sus. AC	Sussex Archaeological Society: Collections (London 1848-).
Sus. RS	Sussex Record Society: Publications (Lewes 1902-).
TFLieb.	Texte und Forschungen zur englischen Kulturgeschichte: Festgabe für Felix Liebermann, ed. H. Boehmer, A. Brandl, etc. (Halle 1921).
TLS	Times Literary Supplement (London 1902-).
TSE	University of Texas Publications: Studies in English (Austin 1911-).
VHCE	Victoria History of the Counties of England, ed. H.A. Doubleday, W. Page, & others (Westminster 1900-).
WANHSM	Wiltshire Archaeological and Natural History Society: Magazine (Devizes 1854-).
War. AM	Warwickshire Antiquarian Magazine (Warwick 1-859-77).
WB	Wiener Beiträge zur Kulturgeschichte und Linguistik (Vienna 1930-).
WBEP	Wiener Beiträge zur englischen Philologie (Vienna 1895-).
WC	Warton Club: Publications (London 1855-6).
Wor. HS	Worcestershire Historical Society: Publications (Oxford 1893-).
WSAS	William Salt Archaeological Society: Staffordshire Record Society: Collections (Birmingham 1880-).
YAJ	Yorkshire Archaeological Journal (London 1870-).
YASRS	Yorkshire Archaeological Society: Record series (Worksop 1885-).
YASRSES	Yorkshire Archaeological Society: Record series, extra series (Wakefield 1935-).
YHP	Yale Historical Publications: Manuscripts and edited texts (New Haven, 1913-).
Yks. CM	Yorkshire County Magazine (Bingley 1888-90).
YSE	Yale Studies in English (New Haven 1898-).

References

Adamson, Sylvia – Vivien A. Law – Nigel Vincent – Susan Wright (eds.)
   1990 *Papers from the 5th International Conference on English Historical Linguistics*. Amsterdam: John Benjamins.

Ammon, Ulrich – Norbert Dittmar – Klaus J. Mattheir (eds.)
   1987 *Sociolinguistics. An International Handbook of the Science of Language and Society*. Berlin: Walter de Gruyter.

Arbman, Holger – Alan Binns (eds.)
   1961 *The Vikings*. London: Thames and Hudson.

Arngart, Olof S.A.
   1947 "Some Aspects of the Relation between the English and the Danish Element in the Danelaw", *Studia Neophilologica* 20: 73-87.
   1963 *Selected Papers*. Lund: Gleerup.

Ashdown, Margaret
   1930 *English and Norse Documents relating to the Reign of Ethelred the Unready*. Cambridge: Cambridge University Press.

Atkinson, Ian
   1990 *Los barcos vikingos*. Madrid: Akal/Cambridge.

Austin, Thomas (ed.)
   1888 *Two Fifteenth Century Cookery Books*. (Early English Text Society 91.) Oxford: Oxford University Press.

Bailey, Charles James
   1973 *Variation and Linguistic Theory*. Arlington, Va: Georgetown Center for Applied Linguistics.
   1987 "Variation Theory and so-called Sociolinguistic Grammars", *Language and Communication* 7/4: 269-291.

Bailey, Charles James – Karl Maroldt
   1977 "The French lineage of English", in: Jürgen M. Meisel (ed.), 21-53.

Barnes, John A.
   1954 "Class and Committees in a Norwegian Island Parish", *Human Relations* 7: 39-58.
   1969 "Networks and Political Process", in: Mitchell, J. Clyde, (ed.), 51-76.
   1972 *Social Networks*. Reading: Massachussets.

Bastardas Boada, Albert
2006 "La evolución de la diversidad lingüística: comprender para proponer", in: Blas Arroyo, José Luis – Manuela Casanova Avalos – Mónica Velando Casanova (eds.), 23-32.

Bator, Magdalena
2009 "Obsolete Scandinavian loanwords in English: A semantic analysis of the field 'people'", *Kwartalnik neofilologiczny* LVI/3: 339-347.

Baugh, John – Joel Scherzer (eds.)
1984 *Language in Use*. Englewood Cliffs, NJ: Prentice Hall.

Beaven, Murray L.R.
1918 "The beginning of the year in the Alfredian Chronicle", *English Historical Review* XXXIII: 328-342.

Bekker-Nielsen, Hans – Peter Foote – Olaf Olsen (eds.)
1981 *Proceedings of the 8th Viking Congress, Arhus 1977*. Odense: Odense University Press.

Bennet, Jack Arthur Walter – G.V. Smithers (eds.)
1974 *Early Middle English Verse and Prose*. Oxford: Clarendon Press.

Bergen, Henry (ed.)
1924 *Lydgate's Fall of Princes*. (Early English Text Society 121 122 123.) Oxford: Oxford University Press.

Berndt, Rolf
1989 *A History of the English Language*. Leipzig: Verlag Enzyklopädie Leipzig.

Bernstein, Basil
1961 "Social structure, language and learning", *Educational Research* 3: 163-173.

Biber, Douglas
2006 *University language: a corpus-based study of spoken and written registers*. Amsterdam: John Benjamins.

Bickerton, Derek
1981 *Roots of Language*. Ann Arbor: University of Michigan Press.

Birdsong, David
1992 "Ultimate Attainmet in Second Language Acquisition", *Language* 68/4: 706-755.

Bjørkman, Erik
1900 *Scandinavian Loanwords in Middle English*. Halle: Max Niemeyer.

1910   *Nordische Personennamen in England.* Halle: Max Niemeyer.
1912   *Zur englischen Namenkunde.* Halle: Max Niemeyer.
Blair, Peter Hunter
    1970   *Anglo-Saxon England.* Cambridge: Cambridge University Press.
Blas Arroyo, José Luis – Manuela Casanova Avalos – Mónica Velando Casanova (eds.)
    2006   *Discurso y sociedad: contribuciones al estudio de la lengua en contexto social.* Castelló: Universitat Jaume I.
Block, Katharine Salter (ed.)
    1922   *Ludus Coventriae or the plaie called Corpus Christi.* (Early English Text Society, Extra Series 120.) Oxford: Oxford University Press.
Blockley, Mary
    2008   "Essential Linguistics", in: Haruko Momma – Michael Matto (eds.), 18-24.
Bloomfield, Leonard
    1933   *Language.* New York: MacMillan.
Boissevain, Jeremy
    1987   "Social Networks", in: Ulrich Ammon – Norbert Dittmar – Klaus J. Mattheir (eds.), 164-169.
Bott, Elizabeth
    1957   *Family and Social Network: Roles, norms and external relationships in ordinary urban families.* London: Tavistock Publications.
Bright, William (ed.)
    1969   *Explorations in Sociolinguistics.* The Hague: Mouton de Gruyter.
Britton, Derek (ed.)
    1996   *English Historical Linguistics 1994.* Amsterdam/Philadelphia: John Benjamins.
Brown, Beatrice Daw (ed.)
    1927   *The Southern Passion.* (Early English Text Society 169.) Oxford: Oxford University Press.
Brown, Carleton – Rossell Hope Robbins
    1943   *Index of Middle English Verse.* New York: Columbia University Press.
Braunmüller, Kurt – Juliane House (eds.)
    2009   *Convergence and Divergence in language contact situations.* Amsterdam: Benjamins.

Bühler, Curt F. (ed.)
  1941 *The Dicts and Sayings of the Philosophers.* (Early English Text Society 211.) Oxford: Oxford University Press.
Cameron, Kenneth
  1953 "The Scandinavians in Derbyshire: the Place-Name Evidence", *Nottingham Mediaeval Studies* 2: 86-118.
  1959 *The Place-Names of Derbyshire.* (English Place-Name Society XVII-XXIX.) Cambridge: Cambridge University Press.
  1965 *Scandinavian Settlement in the Territory of the Five Boroughs: The Place-Name Evidence.* Nottingham: University of Nottingham.
  1969 "The Two Viking Ages of Britain: Linguistic and Place-Name Evidence", *Mediaeval Scandinavia* 2: 176-179.
Cameron, Kenneth
  1970 "Scandinavian Settlement in the Territory of the Five Boroughs: The Place-Name Evidence, Part II, place-names in *thorp*", *Mediaeval Scandinavia* 3: 35-49.
  1971 "Scandinavian Settlements in the Territory of the Five Boroughs: The Place-Name Evidence, Part III, the Grimston Hybrids" in: Peter Clemoes – Kathleen Hughes (eds.), 147-163.
  1977 *English Place-Names.* London: Batsford.
Cameron, Kenneth (ed.)
  1975 *Place-Name Evidence for the Anglo-Saxon Invasion and Scandinavian Settlement.* Nottingham: English Place-Name Society.
Chadwick, Hector Munro
  1907 *The Origin of the English Nation.* Cambirdge: Cambridge University Press.
Chambers, Jack – Peter Trudgill – Natalie Schilling-Estes (eds.)
  2002 *Handbook of language variation and change.* Oxford: Blackwell.
Chamosa, José Luis (ed.)
  1997 *Actas del V Congreso de la Sociedad Espanola de Lengua y Literatura Inglesa Medieval.* León: Universaidad de León.
Chomsky, Noam
  1965 *Aspects of the Theory of Syntax.* Cambridge: MIT Press.
Chrimes, Stanley Bertram
  1966 *An Introduction to the Administrative History of Medieval England.* Oxford: Blackwell.

Clark, Cecily
   1990   "Historical linguistics. Linguistic Archaeology", in: Sylvia Adamason (ed.), 55-68.

Clemoes, Peter – Kathleen Hughes (eds.)
   1971   *England before the Conquest: Studies in Primary Sources Presented to Dorothy Whitelock.* Cambridge: Cambridge University Press.

Clubb, Merrel D. Jr. (ed.)
   1953   *The Middle English Pilgrimage of the Soul.* [Unpublished Ph.D. dissertation, University of Michigan.]

Clyne, Michael
   1987   "History of research on Language Contact", in: Ammon, Ulrich – Norbert Dittmar – Klaus J. Mattheir (eds.), 452-459.

Coates, Jennifer
   1986   *Women, Men and language. A sociolinguistic account of sex differences in language.* London: Longman.

Collingwood, Robin George
   1946   *The Idea of History.* Oxford: Oxford University Press.

Collingwood, Robin George – William Dray – W. Jan Van der Dussen
   2001   *The Principles of History: And Other Writings in Philosophy of History.* Oxford: Oxford University Press.

Cottle, Basil
   1969   *The Triumph of English* 1350-1400. London: Blandford Press.

Couper-Kuhlen, Elizabeth – Bernd Kortmann (eds.)
   2000   *Cause, condition, concession, contrast: Cognitive and discourse perspectives.* Berlin: Mouton de Gruyter.

Crespo García, Begoña
   2012   *A semantic Approach to the History of English.* Bern: Peter Lang.

Czerniak, Izabela
   2011   "Anglo-Scandinavian language contacts and word order shift in early English", in: Jacek Fisiak – Magdalena Bator (eds.), 139-154.

Dalton-Puffer, Christiane
   1995   "Middle English as a creole and its opposite: On the value of plausible speculation", in: Jacek Fisiak (ed.), 35-50.

Dance, Richard
   2003   *Words Derived from Old Norse in Early Middle English: Studies in the Vocabulary of the South-West Midland Texts*. Tempe, Ariz.: Arizona Center for Medieval and Renaissance Studies.

Dance, Richard
   2011   "Tomor3an hit is awane: words derived from Old Norse in four Lambeth Homilies", in: Jacek Fisiak – Magdalena Bator (eds.), 77-127.

Danchev, Andrei
   1997   "The Middle English creolisation hypothesis revisited", in: Jacek Fisiak (ed.), 79-108.

Darby, Henry Clifford (ed.)
   1936   *An Historical Geography of England before AD 1800*. Cambridge: Cambridge University Press.
   1976   *A New Historical Geography of England before 1600*. Cambridge: Cambridge University Press.

Darby, Henry Clifford
   1977   *Domesday England*. Cambridge: Cambridge University Press.

Dawson, Hope
   2003   "Defining the outcome of language contact: Old English and Old Norse", *OSUWPL* 57: 40-57.

De la Cruz Cabanillas, Isabel – Javier Martín Arista (eds.)
   2001   *Lingüística histórica inglesa*. Barcelona: Ariel.

Domingue, Nicole Z.
   1977   "Middle English: Another Creole?", *Journal of Creole Studies* 1: 89-100.

Ekwall, Eilert
   1937-1945   "The Proportion of Scandinavian Settlers in the Danelaw", *Saga Book of the Viking Society* XII: 19-34.
   1963   "How Long did the Scandinavian Language Survive in England?", in: Olof S.A. Arngart (ed.), 54-67.

Elwert, Theodor W.
   1973   *Das Zweisprachige Individuum: Ein Selbstzeugnis*. Mainz: Verlag der Akademie der Wissenschaften und Literatur.

Emerson, Oliver Farrar (ed.)
1905 *A Middle English Reader: edited, with grammatical introduction notes, and glossary.* New York: Macmillan.

Fanego Lema, Teresa – Luis Iglesias Rábade – Amelia Fraga – Belén Méndez Naya – Isabel Moskowich (eds.)
1993 *Papers from the IVth International Conference of the Spanish Society for Medieval English Language and Literature.* Santiago de Compostela: Universidade de Santiago

Fasold, Ralph
1990 *The Sociolinguistics of Language.* Oxford: Basil Blackwell.

Fellows-Jensen, Gillian
1987 "The Vikings' Relationship with Christianity in the British Isles: The Evidence of Place-Names Containing the Element *kirkja*", in: Hans Bekker-Nielsen – Peter Foote – Olaf Olsen (eds.), 295-307.

Ferguson, Charles A.
1959 "Diglossia", *Word* 15: 325-340.
1991 "Diglossia revisited", *Southwest Journal of Linguistics, Special Issue, Studies in Diglossia* 10: 214-34.

Fernández Rodríguez, Mauro A.
1983 "Mantenimiento y cambio de lengua en Galicia: el ritmo de la desgalleguización en los últimos cincuenta años", *Verba* 10.

Fernandez Rodriguez, Mauro A. – Modesto A. Rodriguez Neira (eds.)
1994 *Lingua inicial e competencia lingüística en Galicia.* Vigo: Real Academia Galega.

Fernández Rodríguez, Mauro A. – Lucía Domínguez Seco
1995 *Usos lingüísticos en Galicia.* Vigo: Real Academia Galega.

Fernández, Francisco
1982 *Historia de la Lengua Inglesa.* Madrid: Gredos.

Finberg, Herbert Patrick Reginald
1974 *The Formation of England, 500-1042.* London: Hart-Davis MacGibbon.

Finberg, Herbert Patrick Reginald (ed.)
1972 *The Agrarian History of England and Wales.* Cambridge: Cambridge University Press.

Finn, Reginald Arthur W.
 1968 *Domesday Studies: The Eastern Counties.* Hamden, CT: Archon Books.
Fisher, John H.
 1996 *The Emergence of Standard English.* Lexington: The University Press of Kentucky.
Fishman, Joshua
 1967 "Bilingualism with and without Diglossia; Diglossia with and without Bilingualism", *Journal of Social Issues* 2/23: 29-38.
 1972 *The Sociology of Language.* Rowley, Mass.: Newbury House Publishers.
Fishman, Joshua (ed.)
 1971 *Advances in the Sociology of Language.* The Hague: Mouton.
 1986 *The Fergusonian Impact: in Honor of Charles A. Ferguson. Sociolinguistics and the Sociology of Language.* The Hague: Mouton de Gruyter.
Fisiak, Jacek
 1977 "Sociolinguistics and Middle English: Some Socially Motivated Changes in the History of English", *Kwartalnik Neofilologiczny* 24: 247-259.
Fisiak, Jacek (ed.)
 1995 *Linguistic change under contact situations.* Berlin: Mouton de Gruyter.
 1997 *Studies in Middle English Linguistics.* Berlin: Mouton de Gruyter.
Fisiak, Jacek – Magdalena Bator (eds.)
 2011 *Foreign ingluences on Medieval English.* Bern: Peter Lang.
Flege, James Emil – Grace H. Yeni-Komshian
 1999 "Age Constraints on Second-Language Acquisition", *Journal of Memory and Language* 41: 78–104.
Forshall, Josiah – Frederic Madden (eds.)
 1850 *The Earlier Version of the Wyclifite Bible.* London.
Fowler, Joseph Thomas (ed.)
 1891 *The Life of Saint Cuthbert in English Verse.* Durham: Publications of the Surtees Society, 87.

Fox, Peter Stuart – Dudley Vincent Fowkes (comp.)
  1975   *Population History of Derbyshire.* Derby: Derbyshire Record Office.
Frisk, Gösta (ed.)
  1949   *A Middle English Translation of Macer Floridus de viribus herbarum.* (Essays and Studies on English Language and Literature, 3). Uppsala: Uppsala University Press.
Furnivall, James (ed.)
  1886   *The Regement of Princes.* (Early English Text Society, Extra Series 72). Oxford: Oxford University Press.
  1892   *Hoccleve's Works 1. The Minor Poems.* (Early English Text Society, Extra Series, 6). Oxford: Oxford University Press.
Furnivall, James (ed.)
  1896   *The English Conquest of Ireland.* (Early English Text Society 107). Oxford: Oxford University Press.
Garmonsway, George Norman (ed. & tr.)
  1953   *The Anglo-Saxon Chronicle.* London: Everyman's Library.
Geerts, Guido
  1987   "Research on Language Contact", in: Ulrich Ammon – Norbert Dittmar – Klaus J. Mattheir (eds.), 598-606.
Geipel, John
  1971   *The Viking Legacy: The Scandinavian Influence on the English and Gaelic Languages.* Newton Abbot.
Giles, Howard – Philip M. Smith
  1979   "Accomodation theory: optimal levels of convergence", in: Howard Giles – Robert N. St. Clair (eds.), 45-65.
Giles, Howard – Robert N. St. Clair (eds.)
  1979   *Language and Social Psychology.* Oxford: Blackwell.
Gollancz, Israel (ed.)
  1940   *Sir Gawain and the Green Knight.* (Early English Text Society 210). Oxford: Oxford University Press.
Gordon, Eric Valentine (ed.)
  1953   *Pearl.* (Early English Text Society 182). Oxford: Oxford University Press.
Görlach, Manfred
  1990   "Middle English – a creole?", in: Manfred Görlach (ed.), 329-344.

1992 "Language death and the History of English", *Seventh International Conference of English Historical Linguistics.*
2004 *Text types and the history of English.* Berlin : Mouton de Gruyter.

Görlach, Manfred (ed.)
1990 *Studies in the History of the English Language.* Heidelberg: Winter.

Graham-Campbell, James – Dafydd Kidd
1980 *The Vikings.* London: The Trustees of the British Museum.

Greenberg, Joseph H. – Charles A. Ferguson – Edith A. Moravcsik (eds.)
1978 *Universals of human language.* Stanford, Calif.: Stanford University Press.

Hamelius, Paul (ed.)
1919 *Mandeville's Travel.* (Early English Text Society 153). Oxford: Oxford University Press.

Hart, Cyril Roy (ed.)
1975 *The Early Charters of Northern England and the North Midlands.* Leicester: Leicester University Press.

Haugen, Einar
1953 *The Norwegian Languages in America. A Study in Bilingual Behavior.* Philadelphia: University of Pennsylvania Press.
1967 "Semicommunication: the language gap in Scandinavia", *Sociological Inquiry* 36: 280-97.
1978 "Bilingualism, Language Contact, and Immigrant Languages in the United States. A Research Report", in: Joshua Fishman (ed.), 151-157.
1980 "Language Problems and Language Planning: The Scandinavian Model", in: Peter Hans Nelde (ed.), 151-157.

Haugen, Einar – J. Derrick McLure – Derick Thomson (eds.)
1989 *Minority Languages Today.* Edinburgh: Edinburgh University Press.

Hearme, Thomas (ed.)
1725 *Peter Langtoft's Chronicle.* London.

Henslow, George (ed.)
1889 *Medical Works of the Fourteenth Century together with a list of plants recorded in contemporary writings, with their indentifications.* London: Chapman and Hall.

Herbert, Wayne
   2007   *The Germanic Languages.* Cambridge: Cambridge Univeristy Press.

Herrtage, Sidney John Hervon (ed.)
   1881   *Catholicon Anglicum.* (Early English Text Society 75.) Oxford: Oxford University Press.

Heuser, Wilhelm – Frances Allen Foster (eds.)
   1930   *The Northern Passion.* (Early English Text Society 183, Supplement). Oxford: Oxford University Press.

Hickey, Raymond
   2002   "Internal and external forces again: changes in words order in Old English and Old Irish". *Language Sciences* 24: 261-283.

Hines, John
   1984   *The Scandinavian Character of Anglian England in the pre-Viking Period.* London.

Hodgson, Phyllis (ed.)
   1944   *The Cloud of Unknowing.* (Early English Text Society 218.) Oxford: Oxford University Press.

Hogg, Richard (ed.)
   1992   *The Cambridge History of the English Language. The beginnings to 1066.* Cambridge: Cambridge University Press.

Holmstedt, Gustaf (ed.)
   1933   *Speculum Christiani.* (Early English Text Society 182.) Oxford: Oxford University Press.

Hymes, Dell
   1972   "Editorial Introduction", *Language in Society* I/1: 1-14.

Iglesias Rábade, Luis
   1986   Lengua y sociedad en la corte de Hales Owen (1270-1300). [Unpublished Ph.D. dissertation, University of Sevilla.]
   2011   *Semantic erosion of Middle English prepositions.* Frankfurt: Peter Lang.

Iglesias Rábade, Luis – Isabel Moskowich
   1993   "Applied Historical Sociolinguistics", in: Teresa Fanego Lema – Luis Iglesias Rábade – Amelia Fraga – Belén Méndez Naya – Isabel Moskowich (eds.), 153-163.

1997 "Technical and Colloquial Character of Scandinavian and French Loan-Words in Early Middle English", in: José Luis Chamosa (ed.), 199-207.

Janzén, Assar
1972 "The Viking Colonization of England in the Light of Place-Names", *Names* 20: 1-25.

Jesch, Judith
2001a *Ships and men in the late Viking Age: The vocabulary of runic inscriptions and skaldic verse.* Woodbridge: Boydell Press.
2001b "Women and ships in the Viking World". *Northern Studies* 36: 49-68.

Jones, Michael E.
1998 *The End of Roman Britain.* Cornell: Cornell University Press.

Jonsson, Jón
1915 *Vikingasaga um Herferðir Vikinga.* Reykjavik: Sagnfræði.

Kapferer, Bruce
1969 "Norms and the Manipulation of Relationships in a Work Context", in: Mitchell, J. Clyde (ed.), 181-244.

Ker, Neil Ripley (ed.)
1940 "Unpubllished Parts of the Ormulum Printed from MS Lambeth 783", *Medium Ævum* 9: 1-22.

Kerswill, Paul
2002 "Köineization and accommodation", in: Jack Chambers – Peter Trudgill – Natalie Schilling-Estes (eds.), 669-702.

Kirby, Thomas A. – Henry Bosley Woolf (eds.)
1949 *Philologica: The Malone Anniversary Studies.* Baltimore: The John Hopkins Press.

Kölbing, Eugen (ed.)
1890 *Arthour and Merlin.* (Altenglischen Bibliothek 3.) Leipzig: Reisland.

Kristenssen, Anne
1975 "Danelaw Institutions and Danish Society in the Viking Age: Sochemanni, Liberi Homines and Königsfreie". *Medieval Scandinavia* 8: 27-85.

Kronasser, Heinz
- 1952 *Handbuch Der Semasiologie Kurze Einfuhrung in die Geschichte, Problematik und Terminologie der Bedeutungslehre.* Heidelberg: Bibliothek der Allgemeinen Sprachwissenschaft.

Krygier, Marcin
- 2011 "On the Scandinavian origin of the Old English preposition 'til'", in: Jacek Fisiak – Magdalena Bator (eds.), 129-138.

Kuhn, Sherman et al. (eds.)
- 1963-1984 *Middle English Dictionary.* Ann Arbor: University of Michigan Press.

Kurath, Hans et al. (eds.)
- 1956-1963 *Middle English Dictionary.* Ann Arbor: University of Michigan Press.

Kytö, Merja – Juhani Rudanko – Erik Smitterberg
- 2000 "Building a Bridge between the Present and the Past: A Corpus of 19-century English", *ICAME Journal* 24: 85-97.

Labov, William
- 1966 *The Social Stratification of English in New York.* Washington DC: Center for Applied Linguistics.
- 1972 *Sociolinguistic Patterns.* Philadelphia: Pennsylvania University Press.
- 1984 "Field Methods of the Project on Linguistic Change and Variation", in: John Baugh – Joel Scherzer (eds.), 28-53.

Lehman, Winfred P.
- 1973 *Historical Linguistics. An Introduction.* New York: Holt.

Leith, Dick
- 1947 *A Social History of English.* London: Routledge.

Lewis, Robert E. et al. (eds.)
- 1984-2001 *Middle English Dictionary.* Ann Arbor: University of Michigan Press.

Liebermann, Felix
- 1913 *The National Assembly in the Anglo-Saxon period.* Halle: Max Niemeyer.

Linow, Wilhem – Hermann Varnhagen – Theodore Martin (eds.)
 1889 Ðe desputisoun bitwen þe bodi and þe soule. (Erlanger Beiträge zur englischen Philologie und vrergleichenden Litteraturgeschichte 1.) Leipzig: A. Deichert.
Lockwood, William Burley
 1975 Languages of the British Isles Past and Present. London: Andre Deutsch.
Loyn, Henry R.
 1953 "The term *eldorman* in the translations prepared at the time of King Alfred", English Historical Review LXVIII: 513-525.
 1977 The Vikings in Britain. London: Batsford.
Lumby, J. Rawson – George Harley McKnight (eds.)
 1866 King Horn. The Assumption of Our Lady. (Early English Text Society 14.) Oxford: Oxford University Press.
Lund, Niels
 1969 "The Secondary Migration". Mediaeval Scandinavia 2: 196-201.
 1981 "The Settlers: Where do We Get Them from – and do We Need Them?", in: Hans Bekker-Nielsen – Peter Foote – Olaf Olsen (eds.), 147-171.
Lyons, John
 1968 Introduction to Theoretical Linguistics. Cambridge: Cambridge University Press.
 1981 Language and Linguistics. An Introduction. Cambridge: Cambridge University Press.
MaCaulay, George Campbell (ed.)
 1900 The English Works of John Gower. (Early English Text Society, Extra Series 81.) Oxford: Oxford University Press.
Mackey, William F.
 1987 "Bilingualism and Multilingualism", in: Ulrich Ammon – Norbert Dittmar – Klaus J. Mattheir (eds.), 699-713.
Malak, Janusz
 2010 "The rise of phrasal verbs in Middle English – a case of indirect syntactic influence on word forms". Warsaw Studies in English Language and Literature 1: 199-217.

Manly, John M. – Edith Rickert (eds.)
1940   *The Text of the Canterbury Tales: studied on the basis of all known manuscripts*; with the aid of Mabel Dean, Helen McIntosh and Others. With a chapter on illuminations by Margaret Rickert. 8 vols. Chicago: University of Chicago Press.

Markus, Manfred (ed.)
1988   *Historical English on the Occasion of Karl Brunner's 100th Birthday*. Innsbruck: Innsbrucker Beiträge zur Kulturwissenschaft, Anglistische Reihe Band 1.

Mather, Frank Jewett (ed.)
1897   *King Ponthus and the Fair Sidone*. Baltimore: Publications of the Modern Language Association of America 12.

McCormack, William C. – Stephen A. Wurm (eds.)
1978   *Approaches to Language*. The Hague: Mouton.

McCrum, Robert – William Cram – Robert MacNeill (eds.)
1986   *The Story of English*. London: Faber & Faber / BBC Publications.

McIntosh, Angus – Michael Louis Samuels – Michael Benskin
1986   *A Linguistic Atlas of Late Medieval English*. Aberdeen: Aberdeen University Press.

McIntosh, Angus – Michael Louis Samuels – Margaret Laing (eds.)
1989   *Middle English Dialectology: Essays on Some Principles and Problems*. Aberdeen: Aberdeen University Press

McNeill, George Powell (ed.)
1940   *Sir Tristram*. (Scottish Text Society 8.) Edinburgh: Blackwood.

McSparran, Frances
2006   *MED = Middle English Dictionary Online* – http://quod.lib.umich.edu/m/med/

McWhorter, John E.
2002   "What happened to English?". *Diachronica* 19: 217-272.

Meillet, Antoine
1965   *Linguistique historique et linguistique générale*. Paris: Champion

Meisel, Jürgen M. (ed.)
1977   *Langues en contact: pidgin, creoles = Languages in contact*. Tübingen: TBL-Verlag Narr.

Miller, Thomas (ed. & tr.)
  1959 *The Old English Version of Bede's Ecclesiastical History of the English People.* (Early English Text Society). Oxford: Oxford University Press.

Milroy, James
  1992 *Linguistic Variation and Change: On the historical sociolinguistics of English.* (Language in society 19.) Oxford: Basil Blackwell.
  1997 "External motivations for linguistic change". *Multilingua* 16: 311-323.
  1980 *Language and Social Networks.* Oxford: Blackwell.

Milroy, Lesley – James Milroy
  1992 "Social Network and Social Class: Toward an Integrated Sociolinguistic Model". *Language in Society* 21/1: 1-26.

Mitchell, Bruce – Fred Robinson
  1997 *A Guide to Old English.* Oxford: Blackwell.

Mitchell, J. Clyde (ed.)
  1969 *Social Networks in Urban Situations.* Manchester: Manchester University Press.

Momma, Haruko – Michael Matto (eds.)
  2008 *A companion to the history of the English language.* Oxford: Blackwell.

Montoya, Ana – Isabel Moskowich
  2003 "Thirteen Paston Letters in Search of a Standard", *Revista Canaria de estudios Ingleses* 46: 13-33.

Moravcsik, Edith A.
  1978 "Language Contact", in: Joseph H. Greenberg – Charles A. Ferguson – Edith A. Moravcsik (eds.), 93-122.

Morgan, Kenneth O. (ed.)
  1989 *The Oxford History of Britain.* Oxford: Oxford University Press.

Morrill, Georgian Lea (ed.)
  1898 *Speculum Gy de Warewyke.* (Early English Text Society, Extra Series 75.) Oxford: Oxford University Press.

Morris, John (ed.)
  1978 *Domesday Book: Derbyshire.* Chichester: Phillimore.

Morris, Richard (ed.)
  1863 *The Pricke of Conscience.* (Transactions of the Philological Society.) London and Berlin: Asher
  1865 *The Story of Genesis and Exodus.* (Early English Text Society 7.) Oxford: Oxford University Press.
  1867-1868 *Old English Homilies.* (Early English Text Society, 29, 34.) Oxford: Oxford University Press.
Morse-Gagne, Elise E.
  1988 "The Adoption of Scandinavian Pronouns into English", *Proceedings of the Eastern States Conference on Linguistics* 5: 361-370.
Moskowich, Isabel
  1995a "Language Contact and Language Change: The Danes in England", *Revista Alicantina de Estudios Ingleses* 8: 139-153.
  1995b *Los escandinavos en Inglaterra y el cambio léxico en inglés medieval.* A Coruña: Universidade da Coruña.
  2001 "Morfología flexiva del inglés moderno", in: Isabel de la Cruz Cabanillas – Javier Martín Arista (eds.), 624-654.
  2005 "Scandinavians and Anglo-Saxons: Lexical subtitution and lexical change in English". *Forum de reçerça* 10: 2-15.
Moskowich, Isabel – Begoña Crespo García
  2007 "Different paths for Words and Money: The Scientific field of "Commerce and Finance" in Middle English", in: Isabel Moskowich – Begoña Crespo (eds.), 101-115.
Moskowich, Isabel – Begoña Crespo García (eds.)
  2007 *Bells Chiming from the past. Cultural and Linguistic Studies on Early English.* Amsterdam/Philadelphia: Rodopi.
Moskowich, Isabel – Elena Seoane Posse
  1996 "Scandinavian Loans and Processes of Word-Formation in ME: Some Preliminary Considerations", in Derek Britton (ed.), 185-198.
Muggleston, Lynda (ed.)
  2006 *The Oxford History of English.* Oxford: Oxford University Press.
Nelde, Peter Hans (ed.)
  1980 *Sprachkontakt und Sprachkonflikt.* Wiesbaden: Steiner.
Nevalainen, Terttu – Helena Raumolin-Brunberg
  2003 *Historical Sociolinguistics.* London: Longman.

Ninyoles, Rafael
   1977   *Cuatro idiomas para un estado*. Madrid: Cambio 16.
Ogden, Charles Kay – Ivor Armstron Richards
   1923   *The Meaning of Meaning*. New York: Harcourt, Brace & World, Inc.
Oksaar, Els
   1974   "On Code Switching. An Analysis of Bilingual Norms", in: Jacques Quitsgaard – Helge Schwarz – Henning Spang-Hansen (eds.), 491-500.
Page, Raymond Ian
   1987   *"A Most Vile People": Early English Historians on the Vikings*. London: University College.
Palgrave, Francis (ed.)
   1835   *Rotuli Curiae Regis*. London: G. Eyre and A. Spottiswoode.
Panton, George A. – David Donaldson (eds.)
   1869   *The Gest Hystoriale of the Destruction of Troy*. (Early English Text Society 39.) Oxford: Oxford University Press.
Pap, Leo
   1982   "Bilingualism in need of a Conceptual Overhaul", *Language Sciences* 4: 71-84.
Patrick, Peter L.
   2011   Sociolinguistic Variation" <http://courses.essex.ac.uk/lg232/SocioVarSum.html>
Percy, Carol
   1991   "Variation between *-(e)th* and *-(e)s* Spellings of the Third Person Singular Present Indicative: Captain James Cook's 'Endeavour' Journal 1768-1771", *Neuphilologische Mitteilungen* XCII/3: 351-358.
Perry, George G. (ed.)
   1867   *The Abbey of the Holy Ghost: Religious Pieces in Prose and Verse*. (Early English Text Society, 26.) Oxford: Oxford University Press.
Pintzuk, Susan
   2002   "Morphological case and word-order in Old English", *Language Sciences* 24: 381-395.

Poussa, Patricia
  1982 "The Evolution of Early Standard English: The Creolization Hypothesis", *Studia Anglica Posnaniensia* 14: 69-85.
Power, D'arcy (ed.)
  1910 *Treatises of Fistula in Ano..by John Arderne.* (Early English Text Society 139.) Oxford: Oxford University Press.
Quistgaard, Jacques – Helge Schwarz – Henning Spang-Hansen (eds.)
  1974 *Applied Linguistics. Problems and Solutions. Proceedings of the 3rd Congress on Applied Linguistics, Copenaguen 1972.* Heidelberg: Julius Groos Verlag
Radcliffe-Brown, Alfred
  1940 "On Joking Relationships: Africa", *Journal of the International African Institute* 13/3: 195–210.
Ritt, Nikolaus
  2001 "The spread of Scandinavian third person plural pronouns in English", in: Dieter Kastovsky – Arthur Mettinger (eds.), 279-304.
Robinson, Fred N. (ed.)
  1957 *The Works of Geoffrey Chaucer.* London: Oxford University Press.
Romaine, Suzanne
  1982 *Socio-Historical Linguistics. Its Status and Methodology.* Cambridge: Cambridge University Press.
  1988 "Contributions from Pidgin and Creole Studies to a Sociolinguistic Theory of Language Change", *International Journal of the Sociology of Language* 71: 59-66.
Sæmundsdóttir, Hafdís Rósa (ed.)
  1996 *Grænlendinga saga.* Project Runeberg. http://runeberg.org/grenlend/
Samper Padilla, José Antonio
  2006 "Disponibilidad léxica y sociolingüística", in: Blas Arroyo, José Luis – Manuela Casanova Avalos – Mónica Velando Casanova (eds.), 99-120.
Samuels, Michael Louis
  1989 "The Great Scandinavian Belt", in: Angus McIntosh – Michael Louis Samuels – Margaret Laing (eds.), 106-115.

Sánchez Carrión, José María
 1987 "Un futuro para nuestro pasado, claves de la recuperación del euskara y teoría social de las lenguas", *Revista Internacional de los Estudios Vascos = Nazioarteko Eusko Ikaskuntzen Aldizkaria = Revue Internationale des Etudes Basques* 34: 323-330.
Satchell, Thomas (ed.)
 1883 *An Older Form of the Treatyse of Fysshynge with an Angle.* London.
Saussure, Ferdinand
 1980 *Curso de Lingüística General.* Madrid: Akal Universitaria.
Saville-Troike, Muriel
 1982 *The Ethnography of Communication.* Oxford: Basil Blackwell.
Sawyer, Peter H.
 1969 "The Two Viking Ages of Britain. A Discussion". *Mediaeval Scandinavia* 2: 163-176.
 1978 *The Age of the Vikings.* London: Arnold.
 1981 "Conquest and Colonization: Scandinavians in the Danelaw and Normandy", in: Hans Bekker-Nielsen – Peter Foote – Olaf Olsen (eds.), 123-131.
 1982 *Kings and Vikings: Scandinavia and Europe, AD 700-1100.* London: Methuen.
Schleich, Gustav. (ed.)
 1887 *Ywain and Gawain.* Oppeln and Leipzig.
Serjeantson, Mary
 1935 *A History of Foreign Words in English.* London: Routledge and Kegan Paul.
Serjeantson, Mary (ed.)
 1938 *Legendys of hooly wummen by Osbern Bokenham.* (Early English Text Society 206.) Oxford: Oxford University Press.
Siemund, Peter
 2008 "Language contact constraints and common paths of contact-induced language change", in: Peter Siemund (ed.), 3-14.
Siemund, Peter (ed.)
 2008 *Language contact and contact languages.* Amsterdam/Philadelphia: John Benjamins.

Sisam, Kenneth (ed.)
   1925   *Fourteenth Century Verse and Prose*. London: University College.

Skeat, Walter William
   1911   *English Dialects from the Eighth Century to the Present Day*. Cambridge: Cambridge University Press.

Skeat, Walter William (ed.)
   1868   *The Lay of Havelok the Dane*. (Early English Text Society, Extra Series 4.) Oxford: Oxford University Press.
   1886   *The Wars of Alexander*. (Early English Text Society, Extra Series 47.) Oxford: Oxford University Press.

Small, John (ed.)
   1862   *Sermons of the Gospels, English Metrical Homilies*. Edinburgh: W. Paterson.

Smith, Albert Hugh (ed.)
   1935   *The Parker Chronicle*. London: Methuen.

Smith, Jeremy – Michael Louis Samuels
   1988   *The English of Chaucer and his contemporarie*. Aberdeen: Aberdeen University Press.

Stafford, Pauline
   2009   *A companion to the early Middle Ages: Britain and Ireland, c.500-c.1100*. Oxford: Blackwell.

Stenton, Frank Merry (ed.)
   1920   *Documents Illustrative of the Social and Economic History of the Danelaw*. (Records of Economy & Social History 5.) Oxford: Oxford University Press.

Sweet, Henry
   1958   *King Alfred's West-Saxon Version of Gregory's Pastoral Care*. (Early English Text Society.) Oxford: Oxford University Press.

Taavitsainen, Irma – Päivi Pahta
   2004   *Medical and scientific writing in late medieval English*. Cambridge: Cambridge University Press.

Thomas, Linda – Shang Wareing
   1999   *Language, society and power. An Introduction*. London/New York: Routledge.

Thordarson, Sveinbjorn (ed.)
   Grænlendinga Saga. *Icelandic Saga Database* – http://www.sagadb.org/ graenlendinga_saga.no (accessed July 14th 2011)
Townend, Matthew
   2006 "Contacts and conflicts: Latin, Norse and French", in: Lynda Muggleston (ed.), 61-85.
Trudgill, Peter (ed.)
   1984 *Language in the British Isles*. Cambridge: Cambridge University Press.
Twiss, Travers (ed.)
   1873 *Rerum Britannicarum Medii Ævi Scriptores*. London: Rolls Series, 55.2.
Van Coetsem, Frans
   1987 *Loan Phonology and the two Transfer Types in Language contact (with special reference to Dutch)*. Dordrecht: Foris.
Ureland, P. Sture – Ian Clarkson
   1984 *Scandinavian Language Contact*. Cambridge: Cambridge University Press.
Vann, Robert E.
   2009 "On the importance of spontaneous speech innovations", in: Kurt Braunmüller – Juliane House (eds.), 153-181.
Wainwright, Frederick Threlfall – H.P.R. Finberg (eds.)
   1975 *Scandinavian England: Collected Papers*. Chichester: Phillimore.
Wallner, Björn
   1959 "The Distribution and Frequency of Scandinavian and Native Synonyms in *Kyng Alisaunder* and *Arthour & Merlin*", *English Studies* 40: 337-352.
Watts, Richard J.
   2011 *Language myths and the history of English*. Oxford: Oxford University Press.
Weinreich, Uriel
   1953 *Languages in contact*. The Hague: Mouton de Gruyter.
Wells, John Edwin
   1916 *A Manual of the Writings in Middle English*. New Haven, CT: Connecticut Academy of Arts and Sciences.

Wheatley, Henry B. (ed.)
  1865   *Merlin*. (Early English Text Society 10.) Oxford: Oxford University Press.
Whitelock, Dorothy
  1955   *English Historical Documents c. 500-1042*. London: Longman.
  1987   *The Beginnings of English Society*. (The Pelican History of England.) London: Penguin Books.
Wright, Laura
  2000   *The development of Standard English1300-1800. Theories, descriptions, conflicts*. Cambridge: Cambridge University Press.

Studies in English Medieval Language and Literature

Edited by Jacek Fisiak

Vol. 1 Dieter Kastovsky / Arthur Mettinger (eds.): Language Contact in the History of English. 2nd, revised edition. 2003.

Vol. 2 Studies in English Historical Linguistics and Philology. A Festschrift for Akio Oizumi. Edited by Jacek Fisiak. 2002.

Vol. 3 Liliana Sikorska: *In a Manner of Morall Playe*: Social Ideologies in English Moralities and Interludes (1350–1517). 2002.

Vol. 4 Peter J. Lucas / Angela M. Lucas (eds.): Middle English from Tongue to Text. Selected Papers from the Third International Conference on Middle English: Language and Text, held at Dublin, Ireland, 1–4 July 1999. 2002.

Vol. 5 Chaucer and the Challenges of Medievalism. Studies in Honor of H. A. Kelly. Edited by Donka Minkova and Theresa Tinkle. 2003.

Vol. 6 Hanna Rutkowska: Graphemics and Morphosyntax in the *Cely Letters* (1472–88). 2003.

Vol. 7 The *Ancrene Wisse*. A Four-Manuscript Parallel Text. Preface and Parts 1–4. Edited by Tadao Kubouchi and Keiko Ikegami with John Scahill, Shoko Ono, Harumi Tanabe, Yoshiko Ota, Ayako Kobayashi and Koichi Nakamura. 2003.

Vol. 8 Joanna Bugaj: Middle Scots Inflectional System in the South-west of Scotland. 2004.

Vol. 9 Rafal Boryslawski: The Old English Riddles and the Riddlic Elements of Old English Poetry. 2004.

Vol. 10 Nikolaus Ritt / Herbert Schendl (eds.): Rethinking Middle English. Linguistic and Literary Approaches. 2005.

Vol. 11 The *Ancrene Wisse*. A Four-Manuscript Parallel Text. Parts 5–8 with Wordlists. Edited by Tadao Kubouchi and Keiko Ikegami with John Scahill, Shoko Ono, Harumi Tanabe, Yoshiko Ota, Ayako Kobayashi, Koichi Nakamura. 2005.

Vol. 12 Text and Language in Medieval English Prose. A Festschrift for Tadao Kubouchi. Edited by Akio Oizumi, Jacek Fisiak and John Scahill. 2005.

Vol. 13 Michiko Ogura (ed.): Textual and Contextual Studies in Medieval English. Towards the Reunion of Linguistics and Philology. 2006.

Vol. 14 Keiko Hamaguchi: Non-European Women in Chaucer. A Postcolonial Study. 2006.

Vol. 15 Ursula Schaefer (ed.): The Beginnings of Standardization. Language and Culture in Fourteenth-Century England. 2006.

Vol. 16 Nikolaus Ritt / Herbert Schendl / Christiane Dalton-Puffer / Dieter Kastovsky (eds): Medieval English and its Heritage. Structure, Meaning and Mechanisms of Change. 2006.

Vol. 17 Matylda Włodarczyk: Pragmatic Aspects of Reported Speech. The Case of Early Modern English Courtroom Discourse. 2007.

Vol. 18 Hans Sauer / Renate Bauer (eds.): *Beowulf* and Beyond. 2007.

Vol. 19 Gabriella Mazzon (ed.): Studies in Middle English Forms and Meanings. 2007.

Vol. 20 Alexander Bergs / Janne Skaffari (eds.): The Language of the Peterborough Chronicle. 2007.

Vol. 21 Liliana Sikorska (ed.). With the assistance of Joanna Maciulewicz: Medievalisms. The Poetics of Literary Re-Reading. 2008.

Vol. 22 Masachiyo Amano / Michiko Ogura / Masayuki Ohkado (eds.): Historical Englishes in Varieties of Texts and Contexts. The Global COE Program, International Conference 2007. 2008.

Vol. 23 Ewa Ciszek: Word Derivation in Early Middle English. 2008.

Vol. 24 Andrzej M. Łęcki: Grammaticalisation Paths of *Have* in English. 2010.

Vol. 25 Osamu Imahayashi / Yoshiyuki Nakao / Michiko Ogura (eds.): Aspects of the History of English Language and Literature. Selected Papers Read at SHELL 2009, Hiroshima. 2010.

Vol. 26 Magdalena Bator: Obsolete Scandinavian Loanwords in English. 2010.

Vol. 27 Anna Cichosz: The Influence of Text Type on Word Order of Old Germanic Languages. A Corpus-Based Contrastive Study of Old English and Old High German. 2010.

Vol. 28 Jacek Fisiak / Magdalena Bator (eds.): Foreign Influences on Medieval English. 2011.

Vol. 29 Władysław Witalisz: The Trojan Mirror. Middle English Narratives of Troy as Books of Princely Advice. 2011.

Vol. 30 Luis Iglesias-Rábade: Semantic Erosion of Middle English Prepositions. 2011.

Vol. 31 Barbara Kowalik: Betwixt *engelaunde* and *englene londe*. Dialogic Poetics in Early English Religious Lyric. 2010.

Vol. 32 The Katherine Group. A Three-Manuscript Parallel Text. Seinte Katerine, Seinte Marherete, Seinte Iuliene, and Hali Meiðhad, with Wordlists. Edited by Shoko Ono and John Scahill with Keiko Ikegami, Tadao Kubouchi, Harumi Tanabe, Koichi Nakamura, Satoko Shimazaki and Koichi Kano. 2011.

Vol. 33 Jacob Thaisen / Hanna Rutkowska (eds.): Scribes, Printers, and the Accidentals of their Texts. 2011.

Vol. 34 Isabel Moskowich: Language Contact and Vocabulary Enrichment. Scandinavian Elements in Middle English. 2012.

www.peterlang.de

Jacek Fisiak (ed.)

Studies in Old and Middle English

Frankfurt am Main, Berlin, Bern, Bruxelles, New York, Oxford, Warszawa, Wien, 2011. 240 pp.
Warsaw Studies in English Language and Literature. Edited by Jacek Fisiak. Vol. 1
ISBN 978-3-631-61661-1 · hb. € 49,80*

This is the second volume of selected papers presented at the International Conference on Foreign Influences on Medieval English held in Warsaw on 12-13 December 2009 and organized by the School of English at the Warsaw Division of the Academy of Management in Łódź (Wyższa Szkoła Przedsiębiorczości i Zarządzania). The conference was attended by scholars from Poland, USA, UK, Germany, Austria, Japan, Finland, Italy, Ukraine and Slovenia. Their papers covered a wide range of topics concerning the area of language contact in Old and Middle English from orthography, phonology, morphology and syntax to word semantics.

Content: E. Adamczyk: The English-Saxon morphological interface: Evidence from the nominal inflection of the West Saxon and Old Saxon Genesis · *A. Antkowiak:* Scribal treatment of the (to)-infinitive in the 15th century manuscripts of the three selected tales from Geoffrey Chaucer's *Canterbury Tales* · *M. Bilnsky:* The expansion of ME shared sense/stem (de)verbal synonyms: Patterns of etymological interchange · *A. Budna:* Tracing potential foreign influences on Middle English morphology: The present participle markers -*and* and -*ing* · *N. Filipowicz:* Tracing the origins and fates of African fauna vocabulary in Middle English · *A. Hebda: Onde* and *envy*: A diachronic cognitive approach · *J. Janecka/A. Wojtyś:* In the secounde moneth, that other yeer of the goyng of hem out of Egipte – on the replacement of *other* by *second* in English · *M. Kłos:* 'To die' in Early Middle English: *Deien, swelten* or *sterven?* · *A. Kocel:* Nonpalatalised dorsals in Southumbrian Middle English grammatical words: A Scandinavian influence? · *S. Łodej:* The non-denotational meaning in the domain of clergy: Pejoration of the lexical fields of priest, bishop and pope in Early Modern English · and many more

*The e-price includes German tax rate. Prices are subject to change without notice

Frankfurt am Main · Berlin · Bern · Bruxelles · New York · Oxford · Wien
Distribution: Verlag Peter Lang AG
Moosstr. 1, CH-2542 Pieterlen
Telefax 00 41 (0) 32 / 376 17 27
E-Mail info@peterlang.com

40 Years of Academic Publishing
Homepage http://www.peterlang.com